Christi James

23 Ready-To-Go Lesson Plans
SCIENCE
GRADE 3

www.themailbox.com

What Are Lifesaver Lessons®?

Lifesaver Lessons® are well-planned, easy-to-implement, curriculum-based le[...]
complete materials list, step-by-step instructions, a reproducible activity or p[...]
activities.

How Do I Use A Lifesaver Lesson?

Each Lifesaver Lesson is designed to decrease your preparation time and increase the amount of quality teaching time with your students. These lessons are great for introducing or reinforcing new concepts. Use the handy list below to see what types of materials to gather. After completing a lesson, be sure to check out the fun-filled extension activities.

What Materials Will I Need?

Most of the materials for each lesson can be easily found in your classroom or school. Check the list of materials below for any items you may need to gather or purchase.

- crayons
- markers
- chalk
- scissors
- glue
- rulers
- writing paper
- 9" x 12" construction paper
- duplicating paper
- chart paper
- tagboard
- blank transparencies
- transparency markers
- overhead projector
- stapler

- student dictionaries
- sandwich-size resealable plastic bags
- reference materials on planets and Earth's habitats
- dice
- game markers
- peanut M&M's®
- eyedropper
- vinegar
- paper clips
- rocks
- pennies
- water
- dry sand
- gravel

- drinking straws
- large, shallow box lid
- large paper grocery bag
- clipboards or portable writing surfaces
- flashlight or other light source
- pencil sharpener
- spiral notebook

Project Editors:
Cynthia Holcomb, Sharon Murphy

Writers:
Cynthia Holcomb, Nicole Iacovazzi, Martha Kelly,
Patricia Pecuch, Jan Wittstrom

Artists:
Jennifer Tipton Bennett, Cathy Spangler Bruce,
Sheila Krill, Mary Lester, Kimberly Richard,
Rebecca Saunders, Barry Slate

Cover Artist:
Jennifer Tipton Bennett

Lifesaver® Lessons

Table Of Contents

©1998 by THE EDUCATION CENTER, INC.
All rights reserved.
ISBN #1-56234-244-4

Manufactured in the United States
10 9 8 7 6 5 4 3 2

Weather Watch

It's raining, it's pouring, it's an activity to reinforce key weather terminology!

Skill: Using weather terminology

Estimated Lesson Time: 45 minutes

Teacher Preparation:
1. Duplicate page 5 for each student.
2. Gather a class supply of dictionaries.

Materials:
1 copy of page 5 per student
1 dictionary per student
scissors

Background Information:
The following weather terms will be discussed during this lesson:

tornado—a destructive wind accompanied by a funnel-shaped cloud

snow—precipitation in the form of small, white crystals

hail—precipitation in the form of small balls of ice or compact snow

lightning—the flash of light produced by a discharge of atmospheric electricity

thunder—the sound that follows a flash of lightning and is caused by a sudden expansion of air

cloud—a visible mass of condensed vapor suspended in the atmosphere

rain—water falling in drops condensed from vapor in the atmosphere

wind—a natural movement of air

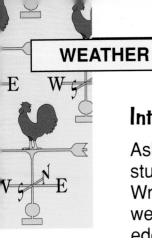

Introducing The Lesson:

Ask students if anyone heard the day's weather forecast. Encourage students to tell the forecast, or to predict what the day's weather will be. Write their responses on the chalkboard. Then have students give weather predictions for the remainder of the week, using their knowledge of seasonal weather.

Steps:

1. Write key weather terms from students' weather predictions on the chalkboard; then have the class brainstorm additional weather words. Record these words on the chalkboard also. Discuss the meaning of each weather word, using the definitions from the Background Information on page 3 if needed.

2. Distribute a copy of page 5 and a dictionary to each student. Have each student use the dictionary to define each weather term.

3. After students finish writing the definitions on the top half of their papers, assign each student one of the four seasons. Then have each student use the appropriate weather words to write a weather report for his assigned season.

4. Have each student cut out his completed weather report. Encourage each student to share his report with his classmates.

5. If desired sort the reports by season before compiling them into a class book titled "Weather Reports From [teacher's name]'s Students."

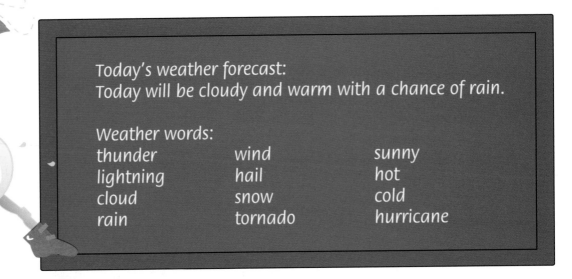

Today's weather forecast:
Today will be cloudy and warm with a chance of rain.

Weather words:
thunder	wind	sunny
lightning	hail	hot
cloud	snow	cold
rain	tornado	hurricane

Name _____

Weather Watch

Use a dictionary to define the following words.
Use the back of this paper if you need more room.
Then write a weather report describing one of the words you have defined.

1. tornado _____

2. snow _____

3. hail _____

4. lightning _____

5. thunder _____

6. cloud _____

7. rain _____

8. wind _____

- -

Weather Report

by _____

_____

_____

_____

_____

_____

_____

Season: _____

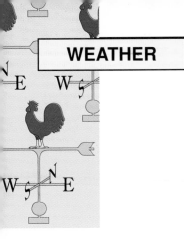

How To Extend The Lesson:

- Have students compare the definitions they provided in the brainstorming session with those found in the dictionary. Ask students to identify the words, if any, that make the dictionary definitions more specific.

- Encourage students to find weather information in the newspaper. Set aside time each day for a weather show-and-tell. Display collected newspaper articles about weather on a bulletin board.

- Share these weather-worthy books with your students:
  —*The Big Storm* by Bruce Hiscock (Atheneum Books For Young Readers, 1993)
  —*Cloudy With A Chance Of Meatballs* by Judith Barrett (Aladdin Paperbacks, 1982)
  —*It Looked Like Spilt Milk* by Charles G. Shaw (HarperCollins Children's Books, 1988)
  —*The Wind Blew* by Pat Hutchins (Aladdin Paperbacks, 1993)

- Have each student make a weather booklet with a weather word, a definition, and an illustration on each page. If desired use copies of the booklet page below.

Pattern

Weather word: _____

Definition: _____

_____

_____

_____

©1998 The Education Center, Inc. • *Lifesaver Lessons*™ • Grade 3 • TEC510

Catch The Wind!

*Students learn to classify wind speeds in an activity
that is sure to blow them away!*

Skill: Classifying wind speeds

Estimated Lesson Time: 30 minutes

Teacher Preparation:
1. Duplicate page 9 for each student.
2. Make a transparency of the
   Beaufort Wind Scale (shown below)

Materials:
1 copy of page 9 for each student
overhead projector and transparency of the Beaufort Wind Scale

Background Information:
Wind is air that moves. It can take the form of a gentle breeze or a raging storm. It affects airplane takeoffs and landings. It affects boats at sea. The wind is important for many reasons, and many people check its status every day. To measure the wind, meteorologists use the Beaufort Wind Scale. This scale describes the effects of wind on the land as follows:

Force 0 *Calm* The air feels still, and smoke rises vertically. (1 mph)
Force 1 *Light air* Smoke drifts as it rises, but flags do not move. (1–3 mph)
Force 2 *Light breeze* Smoke clearly shows the wind's direction. (4–7 mph)
Force 3 *Gentle breeze* Leaves move gently. (8–12 mph)
Force 4 *Moderate breeze* Loose papers blow about. (13–18 mph)
Force 5 *Fresh breeze* Small trees sway. (19–24 mph)
Force 6 *Strong breeze* It is difficult to use an umbrella. (25–31 mph)
Force 7 *Moderate gale* It is difficult to walk into the wind. (32–38 mph)
Force 8 *Fresh gale* Twigs are torn from trees. (39–46 mph)
Force 9 *Strong gale* Roof tiles and chimneys are blown away. (47–54 mph)
Force 10 *Whole gale* Trees are broken or torn from the ground. (55–63 mph)
Force 11 *Storm* Cars are overturned. (64–75 mph)
Force 12 *Hurricane* Buildings are destroyed. (over 75 mph)
Forces 13–17 *Hurricanes* Degrees of hurricane winds (up to 136 mph)

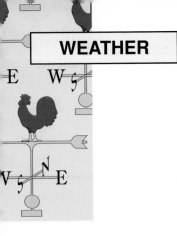
Introducing The Lesson:

Share with students the following riddles: What can be felt, but not seen? What can move a boat, scatter seeds, and wear away rocks? Then explain that the answer to each question is the *wind,* a force that can be both helpful and harmful.

Steps:

1. Share the Background Information about wind on page 7 with your students. Then use the transparency of page 7 to explain the different ways to rate winds.

2. Write the words "breeze," "gale," and "hurricane" on the chalkboard. Ask students to describe each type of wind. If necessary supply them with the definitions shown below.

3. Distribute a copy of page 9 to each student. Instruct students to refer to the Beaufort Wind Scale at the top of their papers to complete the reproducible.

4. Challenge students to complete the Bonus Box activity.

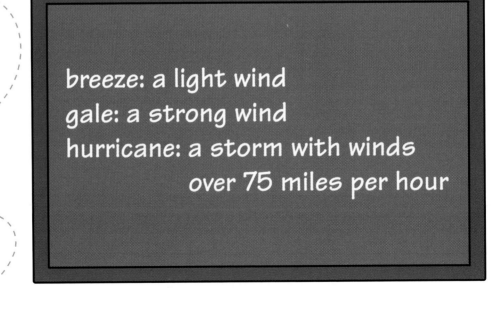

breeze: a light wind
gale: a strong wind
hurricane: a storm with winds
over 75 miles per hour

Name _____

Catch The Wind!

Read the Beaufort Wind Scale.
Name the force of the wind shown in each picture.

Force	Description	Effects	Miles Per Hour
0 to 2	*Calm to light breeze*	The air feels still or barely rustles the leaves.	1–7 mph
3 to 5	*Gentle to fresh breeze*	Leaves move gently or small trees sway.	8–24 mph
6 to 8	*Strong breeze to fresh gale*	The wind whistles and twigs break from trees.	25–46 mph
9 to 11	*Strong gale to storm*	Trees are broken or torn from the ground.	47–75 mph
12 and above	*Hurricane*	Buildings are destroyed.	over 75 mph

1. _____

2. _____

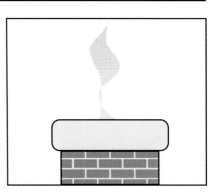

3. _____

4. _____

5. _____

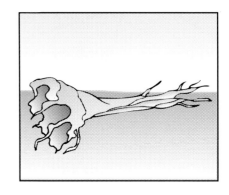

6. _____

Bonus Box: On another sheet of paper, draw a picture of the effects of wind and have a classmate identify it using the scale.

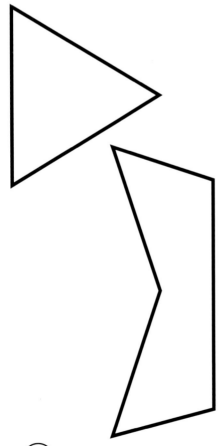

Patterns

How To Extend The Lesson:

• Explain to your students that hurricanes are named by the National Weather Service. This prevents confusion when several storms are being followed at the same time. Each hurricane is named in alphabetical order, alternating male and female names. (The letters *Q, U, X, Y,* and *Z* are not used, since there are not many names beginning with these letters.) Challenge each student to create a list of names for one hurricane season. Then obtain a list of actual storm names for the current year. Was anyone able to predict a name that was used?

• Watch the wind change directions with these student-made wind vanes. To make a vane, each student will need a three-inch ball of clay; a small, plastic container; poster-board copies of the patterns shown; a pencil with an eraser; a plastic straw; a straight pin; a permanent marker; and a small amount of gravel. Instruct the student to assemble her wind vane as follows:

1. Cut a slit in each end of the straw. Assemble the arrow by inserting the cardboard pieces into the slits as shown.
2. Attach the arrow to the pencil by pushing the pin through the straw and securing it to the eraser.
3. Press the ball of clay into the bottom of the container. Secure the pencil in the clay.
4. Fill the rest of the container with gravel.
5. Write one of the following letters on each side of the container: "N" (north), "S" (south), "E" (east), "W" (west).

Take students outside to an open area. Using a compass rose, instruct each student to position her wind vane so that it is positioned in the appropriate direction. Have your students observe the wind direction throughout the week; then have them chart and discuss their findings. Be sure to remind students that the arrow will point in the direction that the wind is blowing *from.*

When Lightning Strikes

Your students will get a charge out of these safety rules!

Skill: Identifying rules for weather safety

Estimated Lesson Time: 25 minutes

Teacher Preparation:
Duplicate page 13 for each student.

Materials:
1 copy of page 13 per student

Background Information:
Many storms produce thunder and lightning. Lightning is a spark of electricity in the sky that makes the air so hot that we can see the heated air. Thunder is the sound given off by heated air. When lightning heats the air, it produces a noise ranging from a thin, sharp crack (if the lightning is close) to a deep, rumbling sound (if the lightning is far away). Since light travels faster than sound, you see a lightning bolt almost instantly, whereas it takes thunder about five seconds to travel one mile.

Although thunderstorms are impressive displays of nature, lightning can be very dangerous. It can cause houses and forests to catch on fire. It can damage power lines so that telephones, televisions, and other forms of communication are interrupted. Every day, someone is killed or injured as a result of being struck by lightning. It is important to be aware of safety rules for this highly charged type of weather.

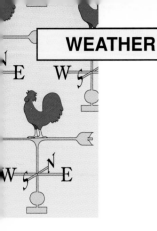

Introducing The Lesson:

To begin the lesson, turn the lights off in your classroom. Tell students that they are going to reenact a thunderstorm. Have one student stand near the light switch. Explain that at your signal, the student will flash the lights on and off to represent lightning. The rest of the class will silently count to five, then clap their hands to represent thunder. Repeat the procedure two or three times.

Steps:

1. Turn the classroom lights back on. Share the Background Information about thunderstorms on page 11 with your students.

2. Discuss with students the safety rules for thunderstorms listed below.

3. Distribute a copy of page 13 to each student. Review the directions together; then provide time for students to complete the reproducible independently.

4. Challenge students to complete the Bonus Box activity.

Protect yourself from lightning! Here are some things you can do:

- When a thunderstorm begins, go inside a house, a building, or a car for protection against the storm.
- If you must stay outdoors, stay away from any large tree that stands alone. Also avoid standing on a hilltop or fishing from a boat. Lightning will be drawn to objects that stand out.
- Get out of and stay away from water. It conducts electricity.
- In an open field, drop to your knees with your head forward and your hands on your knees. DO NOT lie down on the wet ground—it can carry lightning.
- Don't touch anything made of metal. Metal conducts electricity.
- Don't use the telephone unless you have an emergency. Lightning can travel through the telephone lines.

When Lightning Strikes

Unscramble the words in the storm clouds.
Then use the words to complete the weather-safety rules.

1. chout, tlmea
   Don't _____ anything made of _____ .

2. sehuo, rca, idinlubg
   Go inside a _____ , _____ , or
   _____ .

3. yaaw, rtawe
   Get out of and stay _____ from _____ .

4. eret, otllpih
   Don't stand under a _____ or on a _____ .

5. tew, norudg
   Never lie down on the _____ _____ .

6. hoteplene, gcyenreem
   Don't use the _____ except in
   an _____ .

Bonus Box: On the back of this paper, draw a picture showing one of the safety rules.

How To Extend The Lesson:

• Arrange students in small groups and have each group make a lightning-safety poster. Remind each group to include a safety rule along with an illustration on its poster. Display the completed projects in the hallway as a reminder of lightning safety.

• Have students find safety rules for other types of dangerous weather, such as hurricanes, tornadoes, floods, and blizzards. Assign a different type of weather to student partners to research and report to the class.

• Make a graph similar to the one below for students to use to record the weather conditions in your area. After a predetermined number of weeks, have your students interpret the graph to answer questions about the most frequently occurring weather, the least frequently occurring weather, and other weather-related information.

Date	sun	wind	clouds	rain	snow
Dec. 1	✓	✓			
Dec. 2					
Dec. 3			✓	✓	

Month: _____

What Changes

Investigate the life cycles of several different species with this fascinating activity.

Skill: Exploring life cycles

Estimated Lesson Time: 45 minutes

Teacher Preparation:
Duplicate page 17 for each student.

Materials:
1 copy of page 17 per student
one 3" x 12" construction-paper strip per student
scissors
stapler
crayons

Background Information:
All living organisms have a cycle of life. Examples of two animal life cycles are as follows:

Frog Life Cycle:
A female frog lays hundreds of eggs. A tadpole hatches. Hind legs develop, followed by the developing of the tadpole's lungs and its front legs. Then the tadpole loses its gills, and a tiny frog—still with a stump of a tail—emerges from the water. Finally the frog absorbs its tail and can live out of the water.

Butterfly Life Cycle:
A female butterfly deposits an egg on a leaf. A caterpillar, or *larva,* hatches. The caterpillar munches on leaves and outgrows its skin, molting four or five times. Next the caterpillar stops eating and attaches itself to a twig or leaf. Then it molts for the final time, and a chrysalis, or *pupa,* is exposed. Finally a butterfly emerges from the chrysalis.

Introducing The Lesson:

Ask students to raise their hands if they have ever seen pictures of themselves when they were babies. Invite student volunteers to share what they looked like and how they were able to survive (since they couldn't walk, talk, or take care of themselves).

Steps:

1. Review with students the four stages of the human life cycle— baby, child or teen, adult, and senior citizen. Ask students to think about people who are in these different stages of their lives.

2. Remind students that animals, like humans, have life cycles too. Use the Background Information on page 15 to share the life cycles of a frog and a butterfly.

3. Distribute a copy of page 17 and a construction-paper strip to each student. Have each student color and cut out the cards. Next have him set the four title cards aside, then sort the remaining cards into four stacks of life cycles: ant, owl, frog, and butterfly.

4. Next have the student sequentially number each set of cards (in the provided circles), then place each title card on top of its corresponding stack. Finally have the student staple each stack to the construction-paper strip as shown.

5. After students have completed their projects, have each child write a brief description of each animal's life cycle.

6. Encourage students to use their completed projects to share their knowledge of life cycles with their families.

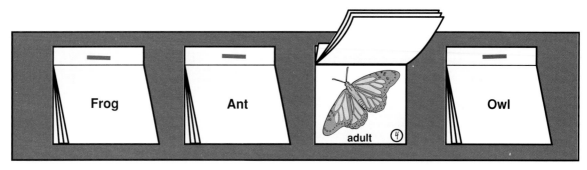

adult	larva	egg	chick
egg	adult	caterpillar	young owl
young frog	egg	adult	egg
tadpole	pupa	chrysalis	adult
Frog	**Ant**	**Butterfly**	**Owl**

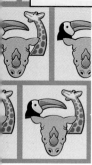

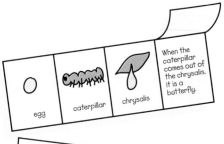

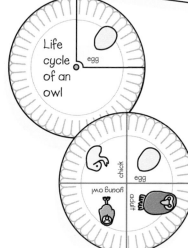

How To Extend The Lesson:

- Have students investigate the life cycles of other animals. To do this have each student choose a different animal to research. Provide a variety of arts-and-crafts materials for students to use in creating diagrams about the life cycles they researched. Some ways students might choose to show their information:

  —**Life-cycle flip books:** To make a book for a four-stage life cycle, a student folds a 12" x 18" sheet of drawing paper in half (to 6" x 18") and makes three equally spaced cuts in the top layer. Then she sequentially labels and illustrates the four resulting flaps with the desired life cycle. Next she lifts each flap and writes a description of the stage.

  —**Four-panel drawings:** A student folds a sheet of drawing paper into fourths, unfolds it, and labels each section with one of the four life-cycle stages. Then in each section she describes and illustrates a stage of the life cycle.

  —**Life-cycle wheels:** A student divides each of two paper plates (or nine-inch tagboard circles) into four equal sections. She labels and illustrates the top-right quadrant on one plate with the first stage of the life cycle. Then she rotates the plate one-quarter turn clockwise, and labels and illustrates this quadrant with the second stage. She continues in the same manner for the remaining two stages. To make a wheel cover, she cuts away one section of the other plate and personalizes the plate as desired. Then she uses a brad to attach the wheel cover atop the wheel. To share her project, she turns the bottom plate clockwise.

- Share the following life-cycle literature with your students:
  —*Butterfly Story* by Anca Hariton (Dutton Children's Books, 1995)
  —*Tale Of A Tadpole* by Barbara Ann Porte (Orchard Books, 1997)
  —*The Life And Times Of The Honeybee* by Charles Micucci (Houghton Mifflin Company, 1997)
  —Life Cycles Series by Sabrina Crewe (Raintree Steck-Vaughn Publishers)

Awesome Adaptations

Explore the wonders of animal adaptations with a look at some fascinating features!

Skill: Identifying animal adaptations

Estimated Lesson Time: 30 minutes

Teacher Preparation:

1. Duplicate page 21 for each student.
2. For each student, program a slip of paper with a different animal name from the list on page 20.
3. Prepare a sign for each of the following habitats: wetlands, drylands, woods, and grasslands. Mount each sign on a different classroom wall.

Materials:

1 copy of page 21 per student
1 programmed slip of paper per student
4 signs, each programmed with the name of a
   habitat (wetlands, drylands, woods, grasslands)

Background Information:

In order to survive, animals must compete with other animals in their living environments, or *habitats*. Animals have special features to help them find food, shelter, and protection. The list below describes some of the special features, or *adaptations,* that allow certain animals to survive.

frog—long, sticky tongue for catching insects
elephant—long trunk for reaching leaves
raccoon—long, flexible fingers for grabbing prey
duck—webbed feet for swimming and diving
eagle—hooked beak and long, curved talons for
   catching prey
bee—thick, hairy legs for collecting pollen
shark—many rows of sharp, replaceable teeth for
   catching prey

bat—high-pitched sound waves *(echolocation)* for
   finding insects
pelican—long, straight bill with a flexible pouch for
   catching fish
anteater—long, slender snout and a long tongue for
   reaching into anthills
spider—ability to spin webs for catching insects
squirrel—powerful jaw muscles and sharp front teeth
   for gnawing through hard-shelled nuts
snake—jaw that can open wide for swallowing whole prey

Introducing The Lesson:

To begin, tell students that they will place animals in their *habitats,* or living environments. Read aloud and point to the mounted habitat signs. Then distribute a programmed slip of paper to each student. Have each student read the animal name on her paper and then stand in its corresponding habitat.

Steps:

1. Have the students in each habitat display their animal names to each other to verify that each student is in the correct area. Collect the paper slips and randomly redistribute them, making sure everyone receives a new slip. Then repeat the activity. Continue in the same manner for a desired amount of time.

2. After the students return to their seats, inform them that each animal has special *adaptations,* or features to help it survive in its habitat. Share the Background Information on page 19 with your students. Then ask student volunteers to identify adaptations of the animals on their paper slips.

3. Distribute a copy of page 21 to each student for her to complete.

4. Challenge students to complete the Bonus Box activity.

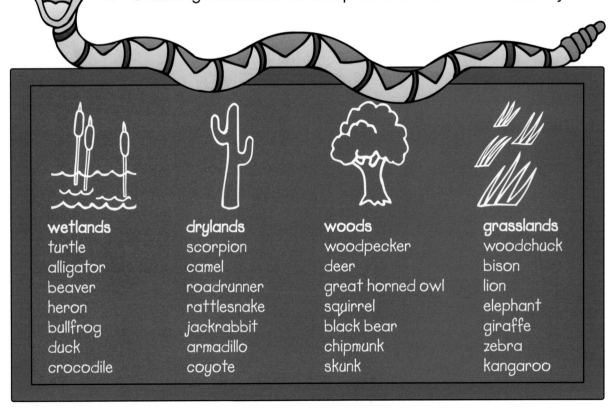

wetlands	drylands	woods	grasslands
turtle	scorpion	woodpecker	woodchuck
alligator	camel	deer	bison
beaver	roadrunner	great horned owl	lion
heron	rattlesnake	squirrel	elephant
bullfrog	jackrabbit	black bear	giraffe
duck	armadillo	chipmunk	zebra
crocodile	coyote	skunk	kangaroo

Identifying animal adaptations

Awesome Adaptations

Animals have special features, or *adaptations*, to help them find food, shelter, and
   protection.
Read each sentence.
Write the matching word on the line.
Use the Word Bank.

> **Bonus Box:** Choose an animal not in the Word Bank. On the back of this sheet, describe how this animal finds food, shelter, and protection.

1. An _____ has a long snout for reaching into anthills.

2. A _____ has webbed feet for swimming and diving.

3. A _____ spins a web to trap insects.

4. A _____ can stretch its jaw to swallow its prey whole.

5. A _____ has many rows of replaceable teeth to catch and eat its prey.

6. A _____ has hairy legs that collect and transport pollen.

7. A _____ uses high-pitched sounds to find insects.

8. An _____ has sharp talons to kill and carry prey while flying.

9. A _____ has a sticky tongue to catch insects.

10. An _____ has a long trunk for reaching tree leaves.

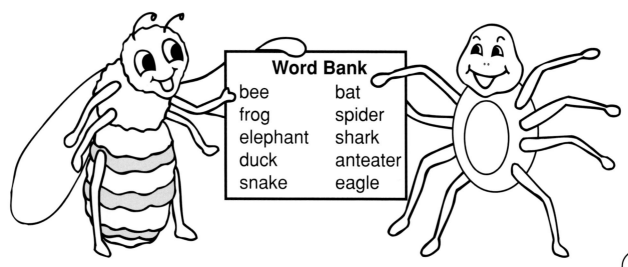

Word Bank

bee	bat
frog	spider
elephant	shark
duck	anteater
snake	eagle

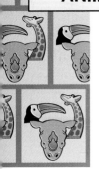

How To Extend The Lesson:

- Have each student select an animal from the lesson to re-search. Encourage each student to prepare an oral report, a poster, or a fact sheet about the animal of her choice.

- From discarded magazines have students cut out pictures of animals and mount each picture on a tagboard square. Place the pictures at a center, and have students sort and categorize them by habitats, survival attributes, types of animals, or eating habits.

- Inspire your students to create imaginary animals. To do this, have each student decide on the distinctive features of two different animals. Instruct the student to draw a picture of an animal with those features combined. To extend the activity, have the student write a paragraph describing his creature. Display the completed projects on a bulletin board for all to enjoy.

The Elefrog
By Calley

The Snabbit
By Calley

The Zebrat
By Bryan

The Pigaroo
By Alicia

The Kitty-bat
By James

Here Come The Vertebrates!

Teach your students to identify vertebrates with a lesson that has a lot of backbone!

Skill: Classifying vertebrates

Estimated Lesson Time: 45 minutes

Teacher Preparation:
1. Duplicate page 25 for each student.
2. Make a chart or overhead transparency of the vertebrate list shown below.

Materials:
1 copy of page 25 per student
1 prepared chart or overhead transparency
one 9" x 12" sheet of light-colored construction
    paper per student
crayons or markers
scissors
ruler
glue

Background Information:
A *vertebrate* is an animal with a backbone. Four main groups of vertebrates are *mammals, fish, birds,* and *reptiles.* The chart below shows important information for identifying the majority of creatures in each group.

Mammals	Birds	Fish	Reptiles
• warm-blooded	• warm-blooded	• cold-blooded	• cold-blooded
• have lungs	• have lungs	• have gills	• have lungs
• have hair or fur	• have feathers	• have scales	• have scaly skin
• live birth	• lay eggs	• live birth or lay eggs	• live birth or lay eggs
• most care for young	• most care for young	• most do not care for young	• most do not care for young

Introducing The Lesson:

Ask each student to put one hand on his back and feel his backbone. Have students try arching their backs, curving their backs, sitting up straight, and turning from side to side while feeling their backbones. Introduce the word "vertebrate" by writing it on the chalkboard. Tell students that animals with backbones are called vertebrates. Ask students if they think they belong to that group.

Steps:

1. Display a chart or overhead transparency of the Background Information on page 23. Discuss the information with your students.

2. Demonstrate how to create four columns on a 9" x 12" sheet of construction paper by folding the paper twice and then unfolding it. Instruct each student to write "Vertebrates" at the top of his paper and then use a ruler to draw columns as shown. Next have him label each column with a different animal group: "Mammals," "Birds," "Reptiles," and "Fish."

3. Distribute a copy of page 25 to each student. Have each student color and cut out the animal cards, then glue each card under the corresponding heading.

4. Display the completed projects in the classroom for students to refer to during your study of animals.

elephant	owl	snake	catfish
shark	Gila monster	seagull	zebra
pigeon	seahorse	dolphin	crocodile
carp	lion	turtle	penguin

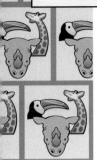

How To Extend The Lesson:

- Provide practice identifying vertebrates with an indoor game similar to Four Corners. Label each corner of your classroom with one of the animal groups discussed in the lesson (mammal, fish, reptile, and bird). Duplicate a copy of page 25, cut out each animal card, and place the cards in a container. Count to ten as each student walks to the corner of her choice. Randomly select an animal picture from the container. The students standing in the corner labeled with the group to which that animal belongs must sit down. Continue play until only one student is left. (When four or fewer students are playing, each player must select a different corner.) Declare the winning player the Victorious Vertebrate; then play another round!

- This nifty idea reinforces the fact that people are vertebrates, too! Distribute crayons and a three-inch, white construction-paper circle to each student. Have each student design a badge to wear that will remind or inform others that people are vertebrates. Encourage students to write messages such as "I'm proud to be a vertebrate!" or "Hooray for vertebrates!" on their badges. Pin the badges to (where else?) the back of the students' shirts.

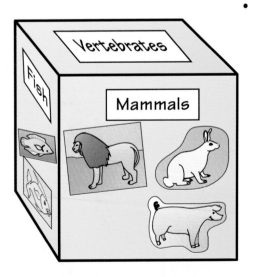

- Have students use a large cardboard carton to create a display showcasing the four groups of vertebrates from the lesson. Cover the carton with bulletin-board paper, and label each of the four sides (not including the top and the bottom) with one of the following groups: mammals, fish, reptiles, and birds. From discarded magazines have students cut out pictures of animals belonging to each group. Instruct students to glue each picture to the appropriate side of the box. For a finishing touch, create a sign labeled "Vertebrates" for the top of the carton.

What Fascinating Creatures!

In this partner activity, students will learn astonishing facts about a variety of Earth's creatures!

Skill: Recalling facts about animals

Estimated Lesson Time: 30 minutes

Teacher Preparation:
Duplicate a construction-paper copy of page 29 for each student pair.

Materials:
1 construction-paper copy of page 29 per student pair
1 resealable plastic bag per student pair
1 pair of scissors per student pair

Background Information:

Fascinating facts about eight creatures:

- **cricket**—Not all animals have ears on their heads. A cricket has ears on its knees.
- **honeybee**—A honeybee tells other bees where to find food by performing a waggle dance in a figure eight. This dance tells the other bees how much food there is and where to fly to find it.
- **anteater**—An anteater can collect 500 ants with one lick.
- **prairie dog**—Prairie dogs kiss when they meet to find out if they are from the same group. If they are, they groom each other. If not, they fight, and the intruder is driven away.
- **lizard**—If a lizard's tail is broken off, the lizard can usually grow a new one.
- **flamingo**—A flamingo is pink because its body takes on the pink color of the shrimp it eats.
- **elephant**—An elephant spends 23 hours a day eating.
- **fly**—A fly takes off backwards.

Introducing The Lesson:

Ask each student to think about something fascinating about herself. Examples might include a time when she jumped rope for one full minute or that she can do a split. Invite volunteers to share their thoughts. Then tell students that many animals have interesting habits or characteristics that they will learn about today.

Steps:

1. Pair students; then give each pair a construction-paper copy of page 29.

2. Share the Background Information on page 27 with your students while they find the picture of each creature on the reproducible.

3. Instruct one student in each student pair to cut apart the cards on the reproducible. Then have each twosome place the cards facedown to play a Concentration-type game. Explain the rules of the game as follows:

    •   In turn each student selects two cards to flip over. If the cards make a match of a picture and its corresponding information, the student keeps the two cards and takes another turn. If the cards do not produce a match, the player returns them to the facedown position and the second player takes a turn.

    •   Play continues until all cards have been matched. The player with the most pairs wins the game.

4. If time allows, pair each student with a different partner to play another round of the game.

5. Have student pairs store their cards in resealable plastic bags for future use.

Use with Steps 1, 2, and 3 on page 28.

A cricket has ears on its knees.	A honeybee tells other bees where to find food by dancing.	An anteater can collect 500 ants with one lick.	When two prairie dogs meet, they kiss to find out if they're from the same group.
cricket	**honeybee**	**anteater**	**prairie dog**
If a lizard's tail is broken off, the lizard can usually grow a new one.	A flamingo is pink because its body takes on the pink color of the shrimp it eats.	An elephant spends 23 hours a day eating.	A fly takes off backwards.
lizard	**flamingo**	**elephant**	**fly**

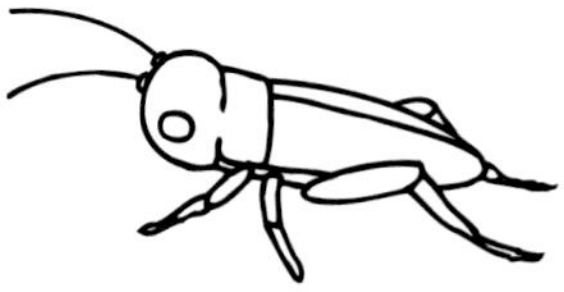

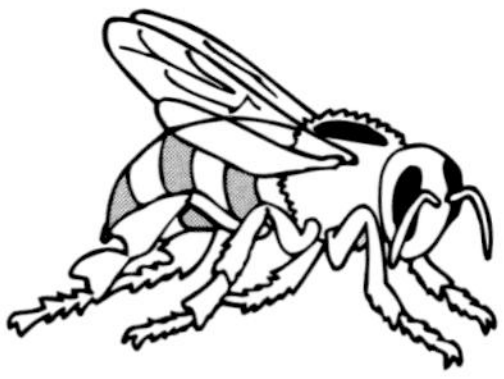

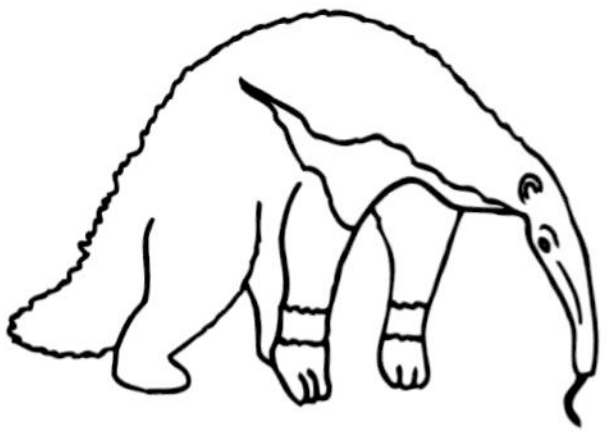

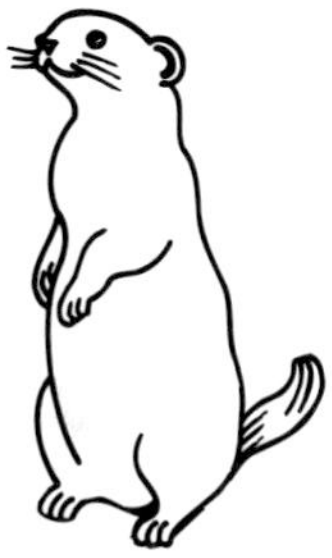

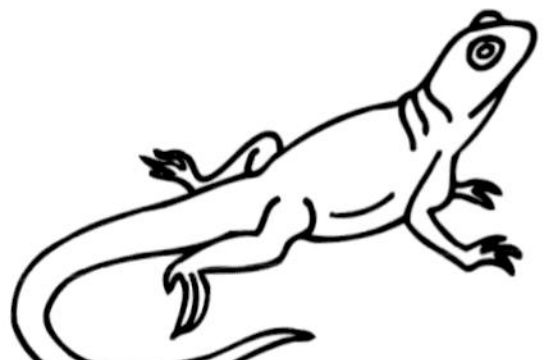

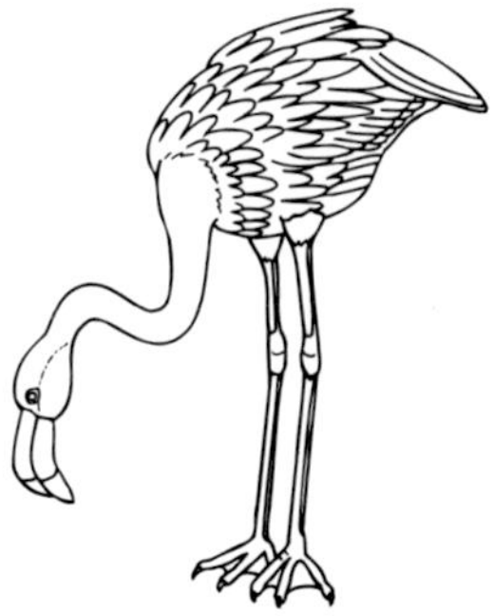

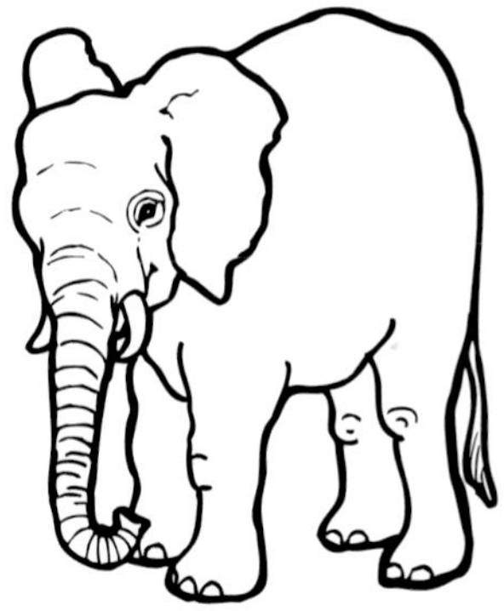

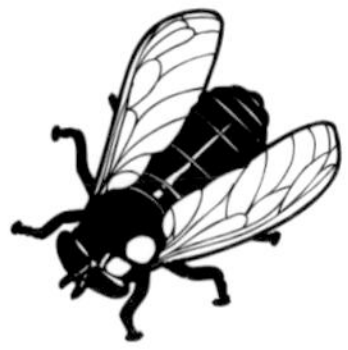

I'm a bird that can turn my head around far enough to see behind me. Who am I?

an owl

How To Extend The Lesson:

• Encourage your students to further research the creatures listed in the lesson. Have each student select one of the creatures and design a shoebox diorama showing the animal in its natural habitat. Display the completed projects in the classroom or library for a fiercely fascinating exhibit.

• Challenge your students to find fascinating facts about animals not listed in the lesson. As each student discovers an interesting fact about a creature, have him create a picture card and fact card to add to the ones used in the game described on page 28. Store the game cards in a learning center for students to use during free time or for review purposes.

• Use interesting facts about animals as a springboard for a writing project. Provide reference materials on a variety of animals, and instruct each student to discover intriguing information about the creature of her choice. Challenge the student to use the information to write a riddle about the animal. To do this, a student writes her riddle on one side of a sheet of drawing paper, then flips her paper and illustrates the answer on the back. Compile the completed pages into a class riddle book titled "Amazing Animal Information."

Cosmic Order

Launch into this solar-system game that will help teach your students the order of the planets.

Skill: Learning the order of the planets in our solar system

Estimated Lesson Time: 30 minutes

Teacher Preparation:
1. Duplicate page 33 onto tagboard for each student pair.
2. Write the name of each planet on a separate sheet of 12" x 18" construction paper.

Materials:
1 tagboard copy of page 33 per student pair
9 labeled sheets of construction paper
1 pair of scissors per student pair

Background Information:
- The first four planets (known as the *inner planets*) are made of rock. The remaining five planets (the *outer planets*) are composed mainly of gases.
- The order of the planets from the sun is the following: Mercury, Venus, Earth, Mars, Jupiter, Saturn, Uranus, Neptune, Pluto.
- Refer to the chart at the right to find each planet's distance from the sun.

Planets	Average Distance From The Sun (in millions of miles)
Pluto	3,688
Neptune	2,794
Uranus	1,784
Saturn	887
Jupiter	483
Mars	142
Earth	93
Venus	67
Mercury	36

Sun

Introducing The Lesson:

Randomly distribute the nine labeled sheets of construction paper to different student volunteers. Tell the class that these students are going to represent planets. Have each student hold the sign so that the labeled side can be read by her classmates. Then explain to the class that they are going to learn the order of the planets.

Steps:

1. Designate an object in the classroom to be the sun. Then, as you share the Background Information on page 31, position each volunteer side by side in her corresponding order from the sun.

2. Ask the student closest to the sun to announce her planet's name. Then have the next student in line announce the name of his planet, and so on, until all nine planet names have been announced. Collect and redistribute the planet signs to additional volunteers. Challenge these students to sequence themselves. If desired, ask the remaining students to provide assistance as needed.

3. Then, to reinforce this information, have students play the card game Cosmic Concentration. Pair students and give each twosome a tagboard copy of page 33 and a pair of scissors. Have one student from each pair cut apart the planet cards.

4. Instruct students to play the game as follows:
   - Spread out the cards and turn them facedown on the playing surface.
   - Students take turns turning over a card to find Mercury, the first planet from the sun.
   - The student who finds Mercury first keeps that card and takes another turn, this time looking for Venus (the second planet from the sun).
   - Play continues in this same manner as students take turns looking for the planet that comes next in the order. When a student finds a correct card, she adds it to her stack and takes another turn.
   - The student with the most cards at the end of the game is the winner.

Cosmic Concentration
For Two Players

1. Cut out the game cards.
2. Spread out the cards and place them facedown.
3. Follow your teacher's directions to play the game.

Mercury	**Venus**	**Earth**
closest planet to the sun	second planet from the sun	third planet from the sun
Mars	**Jupiter**	**Saturn**
fourth planet from the sun	fifth planet from the sun	sixth planet from the sun
Uranus	**Neptune**	**Pluto**
seventh planet from the sun	eighth planet from the sun	ninth planet from the sun

How To Extend The Lesson:

- Display the sentence "**M**y **V**ery **E**ducated **M**other **J**ust **S**erved **U**s **N**ine **P**ickles." Show students that the first letter of each word corresponds with the first letter of each planet in the solar system and that they are arranged in the planets' correct order from the sun. Challenge students to create other silly sentences to help them recall the planets in order.

- Read aloud *The Magic School Bus® Lost In The Solar System* by Joanna Cole (Scholastic Inc., 1992). Have each student write a version of this story in which your class becomes lost in the solar system and has an astronomical adventure.

- Share some out-of-this-world poetry with your students. *Blast Off!: Poems About Space* selected by Lee Bennett Hopkins (HarperCollins Children's Books, 1995) is a collection of poems about the planets, astronauts, and mysteries of space. After reading the poetry aloud, encourage your class to compose poems that celebrate space.

- Demonstrate to students the revolutions of the planets with this nifty idea. You will need the planet signs from the introduction to this lesson and an additional sign labeled "Sun." Distribute a sign to each of ten students. Position the student holding the sign labeled "Sun" in the center of an open area; then place the planets in their correct order. Have the planet students walk around the Sun in a circle at the same pace. After revolving around the Sun once, ask students which planet took the shortest amount of time. Which planet took the longest amount of time? Why?

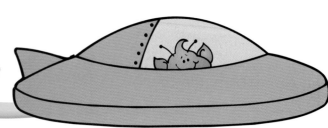

The Planetary Times

Send your students into orbit with this far-out writing assignment!

Skill: Researching planets

Estimated Lesson Time: 45 minutes

Teacher Preparation:
1. Duplicate page 37 for each student.
2. Gather reference materials about the planets that are suitable for your students' reading levels.
3. If desired, post a copy of the Background Information shown below and make a transparency of the diagram on page 36.

Materials:
1 copy of page 37 per student
reference materials with planet information
overhead projector and transparency (optional)

Background Information:
Share the following planetary data with your students:

Planet	Length of day (in Earth time)	Length of year (in Earth time)	Moons	Rings
Mercury	59 days	88 days	0	0
Venus	243 days	225 days	0	0
Earth	24 hours	365 days	1	0
Mars	25 hours	687 days	2	0
Jupiter	10 hours	12 years	16 or more	yes
Saturn	11 hours	30 years	17 or more	yes
Uranus	17 hours	84 years	15 or more	yes
Neptune	16 hours	165 years	8	yes
Pluto	6 days	248 years	1	0

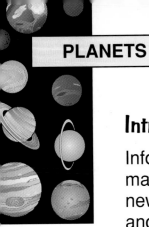

Introducing The Lesson:

Inform students that they will review our solar system in a headline-making way. Ask each student to imagine that she is an interplanetary news reporter. Her assignment is to report the facts, interesting details, and newsworthy data of her assigned planet.

Steps:

1. Assign each student a planet to research. Provide reference materials and, if desired, display a copy of the Background Information on page 35 and a transparency of the diagram shown below.

2. Distribute a copy of page 37 to each student. Provide time for students to research their planets and complete the reproducible.

3. Encourage students to compose catchy headlines for the Our Feature Story section.

4. Provide time for students to share their papers with your class. Then post the completed papers on a bulletin board covered with discarded newspapers.

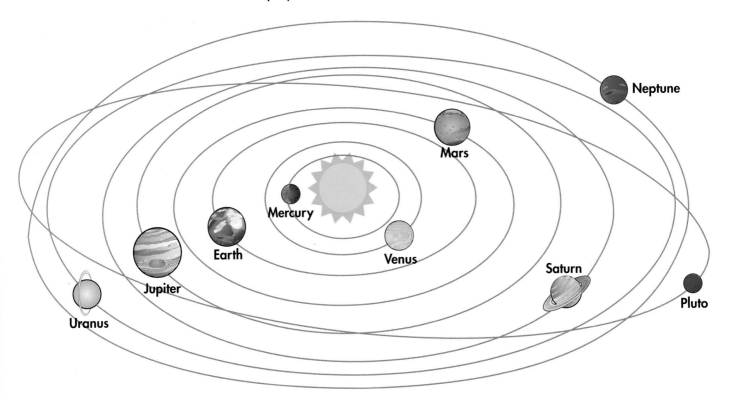

THE PLANETARY TIMES

Issue Published by _____ Date _____

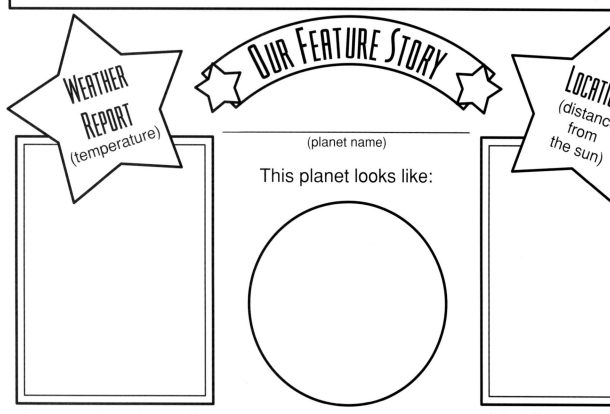

WEATHER REPORT
(temperature)

OUR FEATURE STORY

_____
(planet name)

This planet looks like:

LOCATION
(distance from the sun)

MOONS • RINGS • DIAMETER • GRAVITY • DESCRIPTION • LENGTH OF A DAY • WHEN DISCOVERED

FASCINATING FACTS

1. _____

2. _____

3. _____

4. _____

5. _____

How To Extend The Lesson:

• Integrate creative writing and science by extending the newspaper theme. To do this, challenge each student to create a second page for his newspaper that features a planet-related comic strip, an advice column, advertisements, and want ads. Remind students to use their imaginations—the sky's the limit!

• Challenge your class to use their knowledge of the planets in a guessing game. Have each student write five clues about the planet of his choice on a slip of paper. Then ask each student, in turn, to read his clues to the class. After the clues have been given, have the reader call on a volunteer to identify the planet. If the volunteer answers correctly, he may read his clues to the class. If the volunteer answers incorrectly, have the student call on additional classmates until the correct planet is given. Play continues in the same manner until all students have read their clues.

• Have your students take a comparative look at the planets with a diagraming activity. To do this, pair students, and have each twosome complete a Venn diagram showing how two planets are alike and different. For an added challenge, instruct the partners to compose a report of their findings. Display the completed diagrams on a bulletin board titled "Pairing Up The Planets."

State Your Matter

Capitalize on students' knowledge of solids, liquids, and gases to create a class guessing game.

Skill: Classifying the states of matter

Estimated Lesson Time: 45 minutes

Teacher Preparation:

1. Duplicate page 41 for each student.
2. For each student pair, write a different setting on a slip of paper. Settings might include a birthday party, a movie theater, the beach, and an amusement park.

Materials:

1 copy of page 41 per student
1 programmed slip of paper per student pair
1 piece of writing paper per student pair

Background Information:

- All matter takes up space and has weight.
- The three physical states of matter are *solid, liquid,* and *gas.*
- The physical properties of matter include its size, shape, color, weight, taste, and smell.

Introducing The Lesson:

Tell your students that each one of them has something in her kitchen that can change from a solid, to a liquid, to a gas. Ask students to try to name the substance. After several responses, confirm that the answer is water. It can take the form of a solid (ice), a liquid (water), or a gas (steam).

Steps:

1. Ask each student to imagine the kitchen in her home. Write the words "solids," "liquids," and "gases" on the chalkboard. Ask students to list items found in their kitchens. Write their responses under the appropriate headings.

2. Explain to students that they will work in pairs to brainstorm and categorize states of matter found in various settings. Then they'll use their ideas in a class guessing game.

3. Pair students; then give each twosome a sheet of writing paper and a slip of paper that has been labeled with a particular setting. On the writing paper, have each pair list items found in its setting.

4. Next distribute a copy of page 41 to each student. Have each student write the items from her and her partner's list in their corresponding categories. Then have her use the resulting information to complete the two questions at the bottom of the reproducible.

5. After students complete their reproducibles, have each student pair share its items for each state of matter. Challenge the remaining students to guess the setting. Continue in this manner until all the twosomes have shared their items.

Things Found In The Kitchen
solids
crackers
bread
table
chair
liquids
water
milk
juice
oil
gases
air
steam
nonstick spray

State Your Matter

Read the setting written on your slip of paper.
Brainstorm with your partner different items found in the setting.
Write the items in the correct box.

The Setting: _____

Solids	Liquids	Gases

Answer.

1. What could be found in your setting that might not be found in another setting?

   _____

   Is it a solid, liquid, or gas? _____

2. Would you find more matter in a solid, liquid, or gas state at your setting?

   _____

How To Extend The Lesson:

• Supply each student with a paper lunch sack that has a solid object placed inside. On a sheet of paper, have each student write clues about the object in her bag and tell about its physical properties. Ask each student to read aloud her clues and have classmates guess what is hidden inside her bag.

• Divide a bulletin board into three sections labeled "solids," "liquids," and "gases." Have students look through discarded magazines and newspapers to find pictures of the different states of matter. Then have each student pin his pictures on the bulletin board in the correct section.

• Have students categorize the school lunch menu into solids and liquids. Then challenge each student to create her own lunch menu that includes both solids and liquids. To do this, a student folds a sheet of construction paper in half, opens it, and writes her lunch choices inside. Then she decorates the front cover of the menu as desired. Encourage students, in turn, to read aloud each item on their menus and have their classmates name whether it is a solid or a liquid.

vegetable soup
(liquid)

apple (solid)

roll (solid)

grilled cheese sandwich
(solid)

milk (liquid)

Check Out The Changes!

Help students investigate changes in matter with this high-interest activity.

Skill: Identifying changes in matter

Estimated Lesson Time: 30 minutes

Teacher Preparation:
Duplicate page 45
for each
student.

Materials:
1 copy of page 45
per student
1 piece of scrap paper
per student

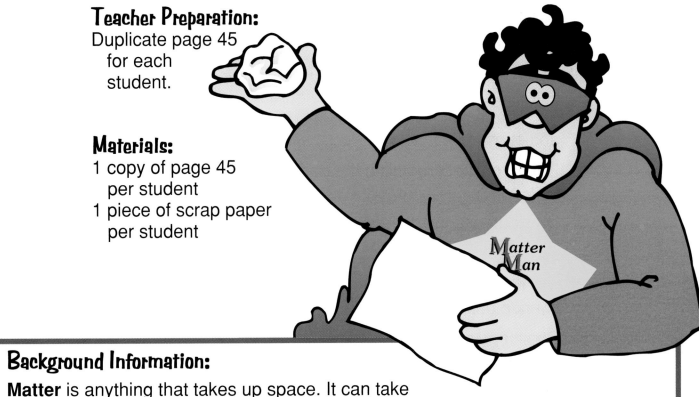

Matter Man

Background Information:

Matter is anything that takes up space. It can take the form of a solid, liquid, or gas. Matter can change in two ways:

• **Physical changes** usually cause a difference in the look or feel of matter, but the molecules that make up the matter stay the same. When a piece of paper is crumpled, it may look different, but it is still paper. Physical changes can include variations in color, texture, size, shape, and form (solid, liquid, or gas).

• **Chemical changes** result in the matter's molecules being altered to form a new substance. When a piece of paper is burned, it becomes ash. It is no longer paper. Chemical changes occur when matter is burned, rusted, or spoiled (as with food).

Introducing The Lesson:

Distribute a piece of scrap paper to each student. Remind students that the paper is a form of matter because it takes up space. Ask students to identify which form of matter the paper is—a solid, liquid, or gas. Then inform your students that there are often changes in matter, which they will help you demonstrate.

Steps:

1. Have each student crumple his paper into a ball. Ask students to list some of the changes they observe. (It changed size and shape.) Reinforce to students that the paper, although changed in appearance, is still paper.

2. Share the Background Information on page 43 with your students.

3. Then tell students that if you burned a piece of paper, that would result in a chemical change. Reinforce that after being burned, the paper is no longer paper. It would change size, shape, color, texture, and substance.

4. Reinforce that crumpling the paper would cause a *physical* change, whereas burning it would cause a *chemical* change.

5. Distribute a copy of page 45 to each student. Provide time for students to read about and identify each type of change described.

6. Challenge students to complete the Bonus Box activity.

Physical Changes
water that has frozen
paper that has been torn
wood that has been cut

Chemical Changes
paper that has burned
metal that has rusted
food that has spoiled

Name _____

Check Out The Changes!

When matter changes only in the way it looks or feels, it is a *physical* change. When matter changes to become a new substance, it is a *chemical* change.

Read about each physical or chemical change in matter. Answer each question.

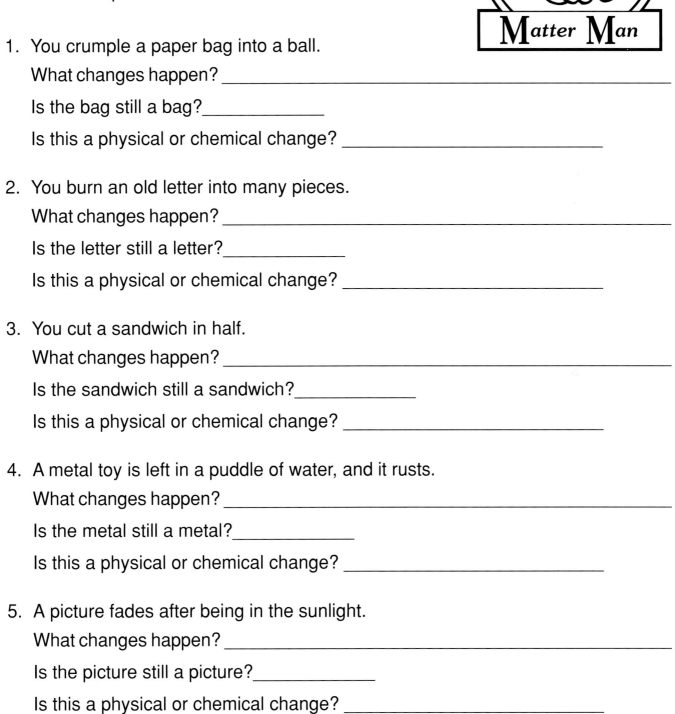

Matter **M**an

1. You crumple a paper bag into a ball.

   What changes happen? _____

   Is the bag still a bag?_____

   Is this a physical or chemical change? _____

2. You burn an old letter into many pieces.

   What changes happen? _____

   Is the letter still a letter?_____

   Is this a physical or chemical change? _____

3. You cut a sandwich in half.

   What changes happen? _____

   Is the sandwich still a sandwich?_____

   Is this a physical or chemical change? _____

4. A metal toy is left in a puddle of water, and it rusts.

   What changes happen? _____

   Is the metal still a metal?_____

   Is this a physical or chemical change? _____

5. A picture fades after being in the sunlight.

   What changes happen? _____

   Is the picture still a picture?_____

   Is this a physical or chemical change? _____

Bonus Box: On the back of this paper, draw pictures to show how a candle, a crayon, and a scoop of ice cream can each be changed.

45

©1998 The Education Center, Inc. • *Lifesaver Lessons*™ • Grade 3 • TEC510 • Key p. 95

How To Extend The Lesson:

- Assist your students in completing these simple experiments to observe changes in matter. Distribute copies of the form below for students to use to record their observations.

  —Place one sheet of colored construction paper in a bright, sunny window and another sheet of the same color in a closet. After three days compare the differences in the two papers.

  —Place one iron nail in a cup of water for a week and one iron nail in an empty cup. Remove the nail from the water, and compare it with the nail that was kept dry.

  —Cut an apple in half and leave the halves exposed to the air for several hours. Cut another apple in half, and compare the freshly cut pieces with those that were left out.

  —Place a piece of chalk and a crayon in separate cups of water. After several hours observe any changes in each object.

  —Place a rock, a cotton ball, and an apple slice in the freezer overnight. The next day observe any changes in each object.

Form

Name _____ Recording sheet

Check Out These Changes!

Test conditions: _____

Objects tested:

Object 1 _____

Object 2 _____

Object 3 _____

What changes occurred?

Object 1 _____

Object 2 _____

Object 3 _____

Matter Man

©1998 The Education Center, Inc. • Lifesaver Lessons™ • Grade 3 • TEC510

Habitat Hunt

From mountains to valleys, and from jungles to deserts, students will explore the characteristics that make each habitat a special place.

Skill: Researching Earth's habitats

Estimated Lesson Time: 45 minutes

Teacher Preparation:
1. Duplicate page 49 for each student.
2. Gather appropriate reference materials for a variety of Earth's habitats.

Materials:
1 copy of page 49 per student
reference materials
crayons

Background Information:
A habitat is a place where plants and animals live. Different habitats include deserts, temperate forests, grasslands, oceans, tropical rain forests, polar regions, and mountains.

Introducing The Lesson:

Tell your students that you are thinking of getting a new pet. You have it narrowed down to two choices—a goldfish and an elephant. Ask students to help you consider which pet would feel more at home with you.

Steps:

1. Record responses on the chalkboard as students consider the environmental needs of each pet. Then ask students to explain why a goldfish would make a better pet for you.

2. Share the Background Information on page 47. Explain that each habitat has special features that make it different from the others, such as the climate, the landforms, and the types of plant and animal life.

3. Distribute a copy of page 49 to each student. Divide students into seven small groups and assign each group a habitat to research. Have each group share the appropriate research materials to complete the reproducible.

4. Challenge students to complete the Bonus Box activity.

Needs for a goldfish:
water
bowl
fish food

Needs for an elephant:
trees
lake
lots of room

Habitat Hunt

Use an encyclopedia or a reference book to find out information about your
   assigned habitat.

Habitat name: _____

The temperature ranges from _____ to _____.

The weather is usually _____ in the summer and _____ in the winter.

Some animals that live in this habitat: Draw the habitat.

   1. _____

   2. _____

   3. _____

   4. _____

   5. _____ .

Some plants that live in this habitat:

   1. _____

   2. _____

   3. _____

   4. _____

   5. _____

The habitat looks like this:

Some special things about this habitat:

   1. _____

   _____.

   2. _____

   _____.

   3. _____

   _____.

Bonus Box: Draw a picture of the habitat on the back of this paper.

How To Extend The Lesson:

- Ask each group to share information about its habitat with the class. After each group has shared, challenge students to compare and contrast the different habitats. Then have students decide which type of habitat best describes their living area.

- Assist each group in finding its habitat on a world map.

- Have each group create a poster or mural showing the landforms, plants, and animals of its assigned habitat. Post the completed projects on a classroom wall; then invite other classes to visit your classroom for a habitat tour.

- Encourage creative-writing skills by having each student design a travel brochure for one of Earth's habitats. Demonstrate how to fold a sheet of drawing paper into thirds to create a brochure format. Have students do the same. Instruct each student to write facts about her chosen habitat on the brochure as well as possible entertainment options and travel accommodations. Encourage students to share their completed brochures with their classmates.

- Reward students for their hard work with personalized copies of the award below.

Congratulations, _____ for your hard work with habitats!

©1998 The Education Center, Inc. • *Lifesaver Lessons*™ • Grade 3 • TEC510

Journey To The Center Of Earth

Your students will dig this game that reviews information about Earth's layers!

Skill: Reviewing Earth's layers

Estimated Lesson Time: 30 minutes

Teacher Preparation:
1. Duplicate page 53 for each student pair.
2. Display the Background Information below on an overhead projector, on chart paper, or on the chalkboard.

Materials:
1 copy of page 53 per student pair
display of Background Information
1 die per student pair
1 game marker per student
1 peanut M&M's® per student

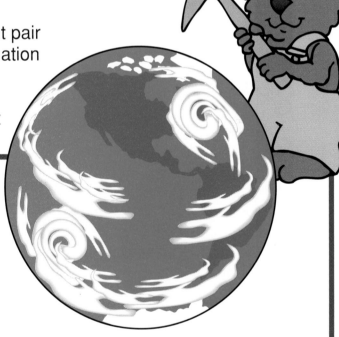

Background Information:
- Earth consists of three basic layers: the crust, mantle, and core.
- The crust is the outermost layer. Its thickness varies from about five miles under the oceans to about 25 miles under the continents.
- The middle layer is called the mantle. It is made of rock and is about 1,800 miles thick.
- The innermost layer is the core. There are two sections of the core. The outer core is believed to be liquid. The inner core is believed to be solid.
- The total distance from the crust to the center of the earth is about 4,000 miles.

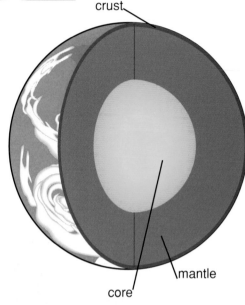

crust

mantle

core

Introducing The Lesson:

Distribute a peanut M&M's® to each student. Instruct the students to carefully bite their candies in half and examine the cross section. Ask students to describe what they see. Explain that the three layers of the candy are similar to the three layers of Earth. The candy shell represents the crust, the chocolate represents the mantle, and the peanut represents the core.

Steps:

1. Invite students to eat their candies as you discuss the Background Information on page 51. Inform students that they will refer to this information as they play a game that reviews facts about Earth's layers.

2. Pair students and distribute a die, two game markers, and a copy of page 53 to each student pair.

3. Explain the rules for the game as follows:
   • Each player rolls the die to determine who will go first. The player with the higher roll takes the first turn.
   • The first player places his game marker on Start and rolls the die. He moves his marker the determined number of spaces.
   • If the player lands on a space with a question and answers it correctly, he stays at that space. (Leave the Background Information on display for the students to refer to.) If he answers incorrectly, he must return to his previous space on the gameboard. If he lands on a space with instructions, he follows the instructions. Either way, his turn ends.
   • The first player to reach the inner core with an exact roll is the winner.

4. If time allows, have students change partners and play the game again.

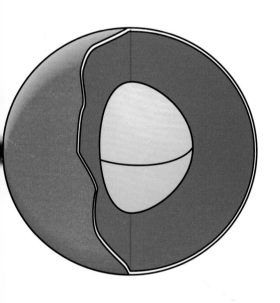

Name _____

Journey To The Center Of Earth

Place your game pieces on Start.
Roll the die and move ahead that many spaces.
Follow the directions or answer the question in each space.
The first player to reach the inner core by exact roll is the
     winner!

Roll again.

Is the crust thicker under the oceans or the continents?

Go back 3 spaces.

What are the three layers of Earth?

Temperatures are near 8,000°F. Move one space ahead!

You have entered the outer core.

How thick is the crust under the continents?

Move ahead 2 spaces.

You are 1,000 miles deep in Earth. Wait one turn to rest.

What is the distance between the crust and the core?

WELCOME TO THE INNER CORE!

What is the outer core made of?

What is the middle layer of Earth called?

You have entered the crust.

What is the mantle made of?

What is the inner core made of?

Temperatures are near 10,000°F. Go back 2 spaces.

EARTH-QUAKE! Miss a turn!

Temperatures at this level are about 1,600°F. Roll again.

You are 30 miles deep in Earth. Wait one turn to rest.

You are entering the mantle.

START

How To Extend The Lesson:

- Provide each student with three small balls of clay in different colors. Instruct the students to construct a model of Earth using a different color for each layer. Then provide each student with a plastic knife to cut the model in half so that a cross section of the layers is shown.

- Have a local meteorologist or scientist visit your classroom to explain how earthquakes and volcanic eruptions occur.

- Make a copy of page 53, and reprogram it with a new set of questions about Earth's layers. If desired, have your students brainstorm a list of questions to use in reprogramming the game.

- Read to your class *The Magic School Bus® Inside The Earth* by Joanna Cole (Scholastic Inc., 1989). After sharing the story, provide materials for your students to make posters showing the inside of Earth. Challenge your students to label the depths and temperatures of each layer.

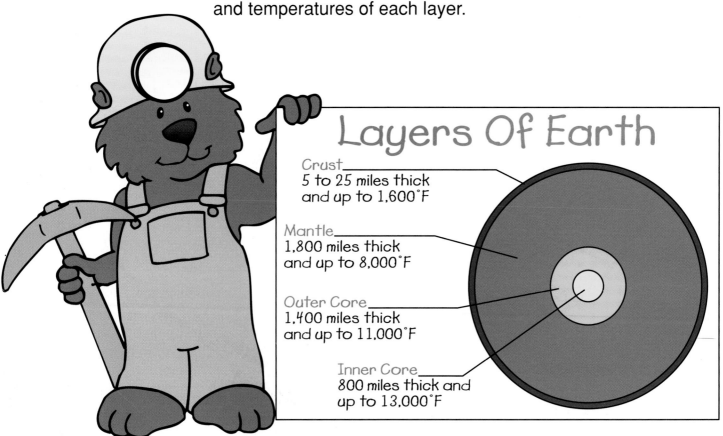

Layers Of Earth

Crust
5 to 25 miles thick
and up to 1,600°F

Mantle
1,800 miles thick
and up to 8,000°F

Outer Core
1,400 miles thick
and up to 11,000°F

Inner Core
800 miles thick and
up to 13,000°F

Rock Detectives

Dig into a study of rocks with this gem of a classification activity!

Skill: Investigating rocks

Estimated Lesson Time: 45 minutes

Teacher Preparation:
1. Duplicate page 57 for each student.
2. Have students go outside and gather (or gather in advance) two different-type rocks apiece. Or provide each student with two rocks.
3. For each student cut two 2-inch construction-paper squares: one from black paper and one from white paper.
4. Set up an area in the classroom where students have access to a bottle of vinegar and an eyedropper.

Materials:
1 copy of page 57 per student
1 eyedropper
1 bottle of vinegar
2 rocks of assorted types per student
2 distinctly different rocks for teacher demonstration
1 paper clip per student
1 penny per student
1 two-inch square each of black paper and white paper

Background Information:
- Geologists measure the hardness of minerals in rocks from 1 (soft) to 10 (hard). Talc has a rating of 1 and can be scratched by a fingernail. Calcite has a rating of 3 and can be scratched by a penny. A diamond has a rating of 10 and can be scratched only by another diamond. The hardness rating of some common materials: fingernail—2.5; copper penny—3.0; and steel knife—5.5–6.5.
- If vinegar bubbles when placed on a rock, calcium carbonate is present in the rock. Rocks such as limestone and marble will cause vinegar to fizz because they contain calcium carbonate.

Introducing The Lesson:

Tell students that they are going to be *rock hounds* for the following lesson. Ask students to guess what a *rock hound* is. Then explain that the term is used to describe someone who collects or studies rocks.

Steps:

1. Share the Background Information on page 55 with your students. Explain that in addition to the hardness of rocks, geologists also look at color, texture, shape, and other attributes.

2. Show students the two rocks you gathered. Pass the rocks around and ask students to observe similarities and differences in the rocks. Tell students that scientists use similarities and differences to classify rocks.

3. Distribute a copy of page 57, a paper clip, and a penny to each student. Also provide students with access to the eyedropper and the vinegar. Have students place the rocks they gathered (or you gave them) on their desks. Review the directions; then have each student complete the reproducible.

4. Challenge students to complete the Bonus Box activity.

sniff, sniff

Rock Detectives

Name your rocks "Rock One" and "Rock Two."
Follow the directions to observe and experiment
  with your rocks.

	Rock One	**Rock Two**
1. Describe the color of each rock.		
2. Describe the size and the shape of each rock.		
3. Describe the way each rock feels.		
4. Scratch each rock with your fingernail, a penny, and a paper clip. List the objects that scratch each rock's surface.		
5. What happens when you rub each rock across: the black paper?		
the white paper?		
6. What happens when you put a few drops of vinegar on each rock?		

7. Complete the following statements:

My rocks are alike because _____

_____

My rocks are different because _____

_____

Bonus Box: Choose one rock. Write a story from its point of view.

How To Extend The Lesson:

- Have students find the length and mass of their rocks. Provide a scale and measuring tape for students to use individually or in pairs.

- Share *Sylvester And The Magic Pebble* by William Steig (Simon & Schuster Books For Young Readers, 1988). Have each student write a story telling what could happen if one of her rocks had magical powers.

- This activity encourages students to explore the benefits of pet rocks. To begin have each student make a pet rock. To do this, a student uses craft glue to attach wiggle eyes to a rock. Next he uses paint pens to draw facial features. Then he adds yarn lengths for hair. After creating and naming his pet rock, have each student create a small poster encouraging others to create pet rocks. Ask students to list several positive benefits of having a pet rock compared with a dog or a cat.

- Have students bring rocks from home. Set up a center with a magnifying glass and a reference book of rocks and minerals. Encourage students to research their rocks.

- Duplicate and personalize copies of the award below for students.

Award

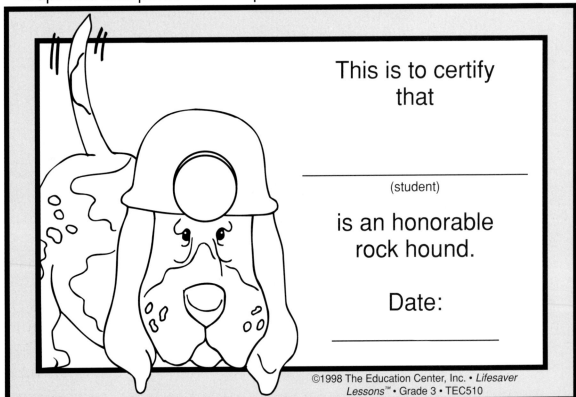

This is to certify that

_____
(student)

is an honorable rock hound.

Date:

_____

©1998 The Education Center, Inc. • *Lifesaver Lessons*™ • Grade 3 • TEC510

Our Changing Earth

Explore the changes to Earth's surface with a hands-on lesson about water and soil erosion.

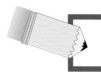

Skill: Recognizing the signs of erosion

Estimated Lesson Time: 45 minutes

Teacher Preparation:
Duplicate a copy of page 61 for each student.

Materials:
1 copy of page 61 per student
1 clipboard or other portable writing surface per student
1 drinking straw per student
1 large, shallow box lid
dry sand
gravel
1 eyedropper
water

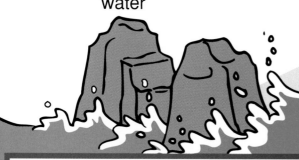

Background Information:
Earth's surface can be changed in many ways. Natural forces—such as ice, wind, and water—continuously wear away, break down, and erode Earth's surface. Ice can form in the cracks of rocks and break them apart. Waves can wear down cliffs. Streams and rivers break off rocks and carry them away. Wind can wear down rocks and move sand and soil to new areas. Because of these continuous forces, Earth's surface is in a constant state of change.

Introducing The Lesson:

Tell students that while they were sleeping last night, there were many changes on Earth. Explain that every time the wind blows, every time a wave hits a beach, and every time the ground freezes, there are changes to Earth.

Steps:

1. Share the Background Information on page 59 with your students. Then tell students that they are going to experiment to see how these forces change Earth.

2. Place enough sand in the box lid to form a small hill. Distribute a straw to each student. Provide the opportunity for each student to blow through the straw at the hill of sand and observe the effects of "wind" on soil.

3. Rebuild the hill; then have the students take turns filling the eyedropper with water and squirting it in the sand to observe the effects of water on soil.

4. Repeat the experiment using gravel instead of sand. Ask students which surface is more easily affected by wind and water.

5. Distribute a copy of page 61 and a portable writing surface to each student. Review the directions; then have students complete the reproducible as you take them on a walk around the school grounds to look for signs of erosion.

6. Back in the classroom, have students share their findings.

7. Challenge students to complete the Bonus Box activity.

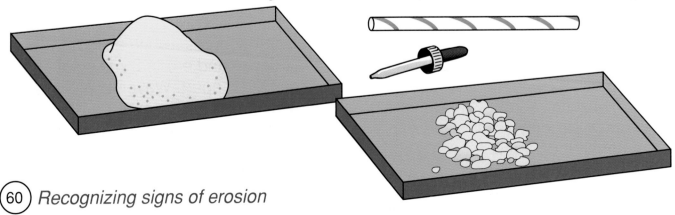

Our Changing Earth

Earth is always changing.
Wind, ice, and water can break up rocks
  and move soil.
When rocks and soil are moved by natural
  forces, we call it **erosion**.

Look outside for signs of erosion.
Use the checklist as you look.
Write down any other findings.

	Observed	Possible Cause
Cracks in the sidewalk	yes ☐ no ☐	
Areas of soil washed away	yes ☐ no ☐	
Smooth, rounded rocks	yes ☐ no ☐	
Water collected in a puddle	yes ☐ no ☐	
Signs or statues that are worn	yes ☐ no ☐	
Paint worn away	yes ☐ no ☐	
Soil drifts against a building	yes ☐ no ☐	
Cracks in the ground	yes ☐ no ☐	
Other: _____ _____	yes ☐ no ☐	

Bonus Box: On the back of this sheet, List some areas around your house where you might find signs of erosion.

How To Extend The Lesson:

- Have your students experiment to see which surfaces are more resistant to water erosion. Have each student fill an eyedropper with water and observe the absorption on a variety of surfaces. Encourage them to observe drops of water on a desktop, a paper towel, potting soil, an aluminum plate, construction paper, a sponge, cardboard, a plastic ruler, and a wooden ruler.

- Have each student write a narrative describing something he left outside that was changed by natural forces. Encourage students to illustrate their stories with before and after pictures.

- Introduce your students to national parks that show signs of nature's forces. Some examples include:
  —Yosemite Valley (California): glacier erosion
  —Grand Canyon (Arizona): water erosion
  —Mammoth Cave National Park (Kentucky): mildly acidic water

- Encourage your students to look for newspaper articles or pictures about how wind or water has changed Earth. Discuss whether each change was a positive or negative one. Post the pictures and articles on a current-events bulletin board.

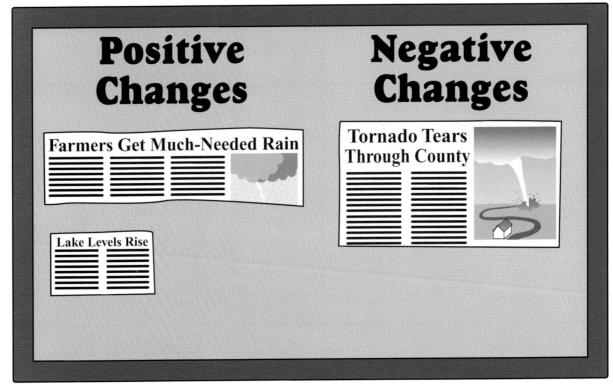

Positive Changes

Negative Changes

Farmers Get Much-Needed Rain

Lake Levels Rise

Tornado Tears Through County

It's Simply Simple Machines!

Take your students on a school tour in search of the six types of simple machines.

Skill: Identifying simple machines

Estimated Lesson Time: 45 minutes

Teacher Preparation:
1. Duplicate page 65 for each student.
2. Gather the materials listed below.

Materials:
1 copy of page 65 per student
2 crayons per student
1 textbook per student
1 ruler per student
1 pencil per student
1 clipboard or book per student

Background Information:
There are six different simple machines that help people work.

- **Lever:** A stiff bar that rests on a support (or fulcrum). It lifts or moves loads.

- **Wheel And Axle:** A wheel with a rod (axle) going through its center. Both parts work together to lift or move loads.

- **Pulley:** A grooved wheel with a rope or cable around it. It moves things up, down, or across.

- **Inclined Plane:** A slanting surface used to connect a lower surface to a higher surface. Objects move up or down on it.

- **Wedge:** An object with at least one slanting side that ends in a sharp edge. It cuts or splits an object apart.

- **Screw:** An inclined plane wrapped around in a spiral. It holds things together or lifts.

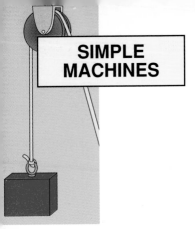

SIMPLE MACHINES

Introducing The Lesson:

Tell students that they are going to work with machines today—simple machines. Explain that a machine does not have to be a complicated contraption with many parts powered by electricity. In fact all complex machines are based in some way on six types of simple machines. Simple machines make work easier. To observe a simple machine in action, each student will need two crayons and a textbook.

Steps:

1. Have each student place the textbook on the left side of her desk. Instruct her to move it to the right by pushing on it. Ask students if they can feel the *friction* of the book against the desk.

2. Next have each student place two crayons underneath the book. Have each student try moving the book again, this time with the aid of two crayon "wheels" under the book. Explain to students that a *wheel* is a machine that makes work easier.

3. Have students observe another example of a simple machine. Tell each student to place one of the crayons by the edge of her textbook. Instruct the student to roll the crayon to the top cover of the book.

4. Distribute a ruler to each student. Have each student place the ruler on the edge of the book to make a ramp. Tell students to roll their crayons up the ramps to get to the top covers of the books. Explain that the ruler acted as another simple machine, an *inclined plane,* to make the work easier.

5. Share the Background Information on page 63 with your students. After describing the six different simple machines, tell students that they will go on a walking tour around the school in search of simple machines.

6. Distribute a copy of page 65 to each student. Instruct the student to take the paper, a pencil, and a clipboard or book (to use as a writing surface) on the walking tour.

7. Walk with your students around the school grounds as they look for and record examples of simple machines.

8. Back in the classroom, challenge students to complete the Bonus Box activity.

Did your students find some of these simple machines around your classroom or school?

Lever: seesaw, hammer claw, shovel
Wheel And Axle: wagon, rolling pin, car, book cart
Pulley: flagpole, window blinds, stage curtains
Inclined Plane: slide, wheelchair ramp
Wedge: plastic knife, nail, fork, plastic needle
Screw: water faucet, jar lid, fan, plastic bolt

Name _____

It's Simply Simple Machines!

Simple machines make work easier for us.
Look for examples of the simple machines labeled in the boxes.
Write the examples that you find.

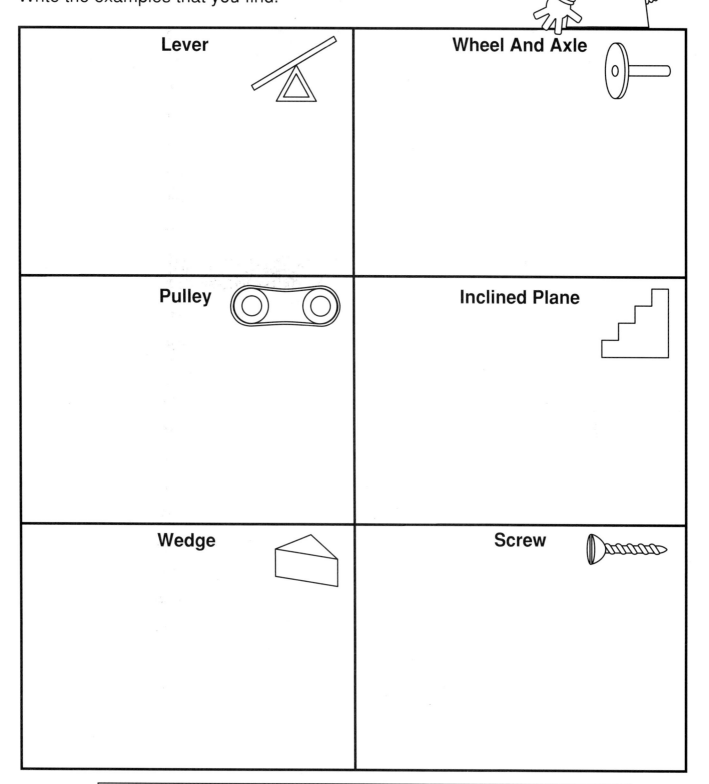

Lever	**Wheel And Axle**
Pulley	**Inclined Plane**
Wedge	**Screw**

Bonus Box: On the back of this paper, draw an example of each of three simple machines you have at home.

How To Extend The Lesson:

• Have students create posters recognizing the six simple machines. To begin divide students in six small groups and assign each group a different simple machine. Provide each group with a sheet of poster board, glue, scissors, and discarded magazines. Instruct each group to look through the magazines for examples of its assigned simple machine. Have each group cut out and glue its findings to the poster board; then display the completed creations for the class to refer to during your study of simple machines.

• Incorporate creative writing into your study of simple machines. Distribute a sheet of drawing paper to each student. Have the student design an invention using two or more simple machines, then write a paragraph describing the invention and what it does. Provide time for students to share their creations with the class.

• Reinforce the six simple machines with a game of Concentration. Pair students and distribute 12 index cards to each pair. Instruct the twosome to write the name of a different simple machine on each of the first six cards, then list an example or draw a picture of each of the corresponding machines on the remaining six cards. Have the partners shuffle the completed cards and place them facedown. In turn each student turns over two cards, trying to match a simple machine name with its example or picture. If a match is made, the student keeps the cards and takes another turn. If the cards do not match, the student returns them to their positions, facedown, and his partner takes a turn. Play continues until all cards have been matched. The student with the most cards wins!

Looking Into Light

Fascinate your young scientists with this enlightening lesson on light!

Skill: Identifying transparent, translucent, and opaque objects

Estimated Lesson Time: 30 minutes

Teacher Preparation:
Duplicate page 69 for each student.

Materials:
1 copy of page 69 per student
1 translucent object, 1 opaque object, and 1 transparent object (See examples listed below for suggestions.)
flashlight (optional) or another light source

Background Information:
- Light travels in a straight line when nothing is in its way. When the light is blocked, it stops traveling forward. Objects that block light are called *opaque.* When light meets an opaque surface, it is reflected or absorbed—or a combination of both. (Examples: cardboard, aluminum foil, a brick, wood, metal)
- Objects that let some light pass through them are *translucent,* meaning you can't really see through them, but when you shine a light on them, the light comes through. (Examples: paper towel, tissue paper, waxed paper, lamp shade, clouds)
- Objects that let rays of light pass through them easily are *transparent,* meaning you can see through them. (Examples: clean air, clean water, clear glass, plastic wrap)

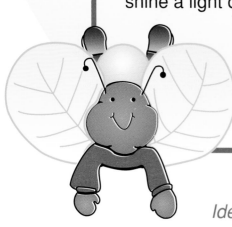

Identifying transparent, translucent, and opaque objects

Introducing The Lesson:

If it is a sunny day, take students outside and have them observe their shadows. (If the weather does not permit this activity, ask students to recall what their shadows look like and how they occur.) Then tell students that although their bodies cast shadows, not all objects create shadows.

Steps:

1. Share the Background Information about transparent, translucent, and opaque objects on page 67.

2. Show students the three objects you gathered (see the materials list on page 67). For each object ask students to predict if a lot of light, a little light, or no light at all will go through it. Then turn off the lights and darken the room. One at a time, hold each object in front of the flashlight (or up to another light), and have students check their predictions.

3. Distribute page 69 to each student. Provide time for each student to complete the reproducible.

Identifying transparent, translucent, and opaque objects

Name _____

Looking Into Light

Objects that allow a lot of light to pass through them are *transparent*.
Objects that allow some light to pass through them are *translucent*.
Objects that do not let any light pass through them are *opaque*.

Read the words and phrases in the Word Bank below.
Write each word or phrase in the correct column to show how much light
passes through the item.

Transparent	Translucent	Opaque

Word Bank

waxed paper
paper towel
cardboard
clean water
aluminum foil
clear glass
plastic wrap
tissue paper
wood
black poster board
cloud
clean air

List five other items below.
For each one, write if it is transparent, translucent, or
opaque.

Example: lamp shade–translucent

1. _____

2. _____

3. _____

4. _____

5. _____

How To Extend The Lesson:

- Use the following experiments to show students how objects can change their *opacity:*
  - Hold an uninflated balloon up to the light and ask students if they can see through it *(no; it appears opaque).* Then ask students to predict whether they would be able to see through the balloon if it were blown up. After taking a class poll, blow up the balloon and have students look at it. Students will be amazed to see that the balloon is now translucent: they can see some light pass through it.
  - Hold one piece of tissue paper to the light and ask students if they can see through it. Then place several sheets of tissue paper atop the first sheet and hold this stack to the light. Students will realize that they cannot see through several layers of tissue paper.

- Reinforce the concept of *shadows* with this bright activity. Set up an overhead projector and gather a variety of small, opaque objects that make interesting shadows, such as a paper clip, scissors, a key, and a bottle of glue. To begin, remind students that some objects block light completely, creating shadows of the objects. Then have students close their eyes as you place one of the objects on the overhead projector. Wrap pieces of tagboard or other suitable material around the projector's tray to block students' view of the object. Project it on the screen. Next have students open their eyes and guess what object is making the shadow on the screen. Allow several guesses before revealing the object. Continue in this manner for each object.

- Invite students to make shadow figures. To do this, set up a projector screen or mount a large sheet of white bulletin-board paper on the wall. Then shine a bright light on the screen. Teach students how to make the shadow figures shown ; then encourage them to experiment with the light to create their own shadow figures.

Quacking Duck

Flying Bird

Crocodile

Identifying transparent, translucent, and opaque objects

Sound Investigations

Your students will be all ears as they try to identify the sources of different sounds.

Skill: Identifying sources of sounds

Estimated Lesson Time: 30 minutes

Teacher Preparation:
Duplicate page 73 for each student.

Materials:
1 copy of page 73 per student
several sheets of duplicating
    paper
1 large paper grocery bag
scissors
stapler
pencil sharpener
pencil
spiral notebook

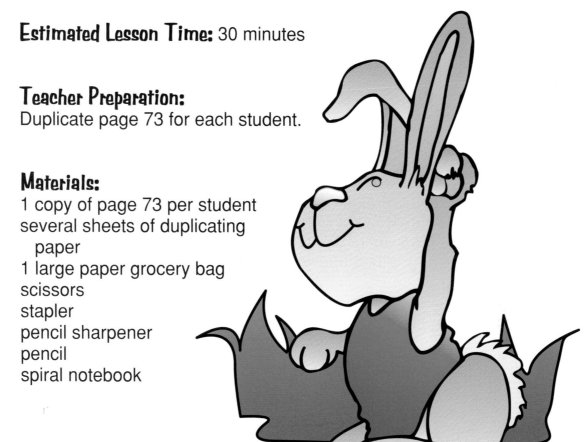

Background Information:
Sound is produced by the vibrations of an object. When an object vibrates, the object causes the molecules in the air to start vibrating. The *vibrations* (or *sound waves*) move outward in all directions from the object. These vibrations enter your ears, and your ears convert them to *nerve impulses.* The nerve impulses are then relayed to your brain, where they are interpreted as sounds.

Introducing The Lesson:

Tell your students to close their eyes and listen very carefully. Walk to one side of the classroom and clap your hands together three times. Move back to your original position and ask students to open their eyes. Ask them if they can identify the sound they heard while their eyes were closed. Confirm that the sound was clapping. Then ask students if they can determine where you were standing when you clapped your hands. Confirm the answer by again moving to that side of the classroom and clapping your hands.

Steps:

1. Tell students that although they could not see where you were or what you were doing, their ears were able to provide them with information. Share the Background Information on page 71 to explain how we hear sounds.

2. Distribute a copy of page 73 to each student. Read the directions with students.

   A. To begin, direct students to close their eyes. Crumple a sheet of paper; then hide it in the grocery bag. Ask students to open their eyes and write on the reproducible what they think the sound was.

   B. Repeat this procedure for 2 through 8 on the reproducible. Some sounds you could make include the following:
      - tearing a sheet of paper
      - cutting paper with scissors
      - stapling a sheet of paper
      - dropping a ball of paper on the floor
      - sharpening a pencil
      - tearing paper from a spiral notebook
      - closing a door

3. When you have finished, ask students to share their guesses for each sound; then show them how each sound was made. Have each student record this answer in the second column on his paper.

4. Challenge students to complete the Bonus Box activity.

Sound Investigations

Close your eyes and listen carefully to each sound.
At your teacher's signal, open your eyes and write what you
  think you heard.
Then discuss your answers and write what made each sound.

What I Think I Heard	What Really Made The Sound
1.	
2.	
3.	
4.	
5.	
6.	
7.	
8.	

Bonus Box: Close your eyes and listen to the sounds in the classroom. Then open your eyes and on the back of this paper, write five different sounds that you heard.

73

How To Extend The Lesson:

• Repeat the activity using the reproducible on page 73 that is described on page 72, but use a different series of sounds. Or, if desired, ask student volunteers to create sounds for this extension. Have the class again record their impressions and the actual sounds on additional copies of page 73.

• Take your students outside, and have them close their eyes and listen to the different sounds. After three minutes have passed, ask students to open their eyes and identify as many sounds that they heard as they can. Repeat the activity in a variety of settings, such as the cafeteria, the playground, the library, the gymnasium, and the hallway.

• Play a portion of a videotape for your students; then turn off the tape and have them list (on provided paper) the background noises they heard. Rewind the tape, and instruct the students to keep their eyes closed and listen again for background noises in the movie. Next have your students open their eyes and list the different sounds they heard. Ask your students to determine if the noises were as noticeable when they were both watching and listening at the same time as they were when students listened with their eyes closed.

• Have your students create a sound-effects recording on a cassette tape. Challenge them to find a way to simulate thunder, a horse galloping, ocean waves, rain, or the wind blowing. Extend the activity by challenging your students to write a dialogue or play that incorporates the sound effects. If desired, have students perform what they wrote complete with the sound effects.

That's Nurse Linda!

• Share *Science Magic With Sound* by Chris Oxlade (Barron's Educational Series, Inc.; 1994). Students are sure to enjoy trying the entertaining magic tricks that use sound as the trickster. Each trick includes directions for preparing and performing the trick, as well as a scientific explanation.

Good morning, third graders!

• Tape-record voices of teachers and other faculty members. Play this tape for your class and have students try to identify each voice on the tape.

Hot Stuff!

Warm up your students with this red-hot activity for recognizing different sources of heat!

Skill: Identifying sources of heat

Estimated Lesson Time: 30 minutes

Teacher Preparation:
Duplicate page 77 for each student.

Materials:
1 copy of page 77 per student
scissors
glue

Background Information:
There are two main sources of heat: *natural* and *man-made.* Natural sources include sunshine, volcanoes, hot springs, and lightning. Man-made sources include heat caused by friction (striking a match, running a car engine) and heat harnessed from the flow of electrons (almost all electrical appliances). Both sources of heat are important to people, for without harnessed heat, we would not have the convenience of modern appliances. Without natural heat, we would really be in trouble since we depend on the sun to keep our planet warm enough to live on!

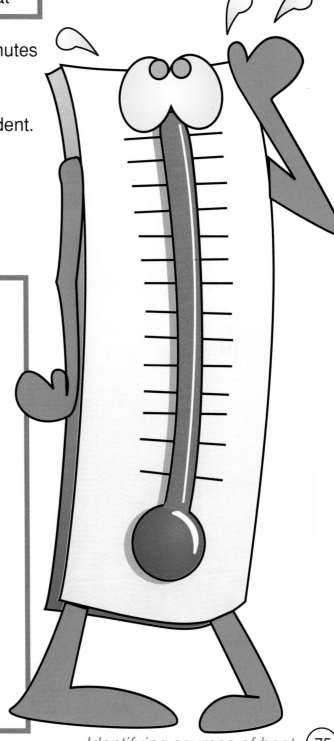

Introducing The Lesson:

Get your class all warmed up for the lesson by having them generate a little heat. Tell your students to place their hands with their palms together and quickly rub them back and forth. Ask students to describe what happens to their hands; then confirm that heat is generated.

Steps:

1. Explain that there are two main sources of heat: *natural* and *man-made.* Ask students to guess which type of heat was created by rubbing their hands together *(man-made).*

2. Share the Background Information on page 75 with your students. Then ask them to brainstorm different sources of heat while you record their answers on the chalkboard as shown.

3. Distribute a copy of page 77 to each student. Instruct students to cut out and glue each source of heat in its corresponding column.

4. Challenge students to complete the Bonus Box activity.

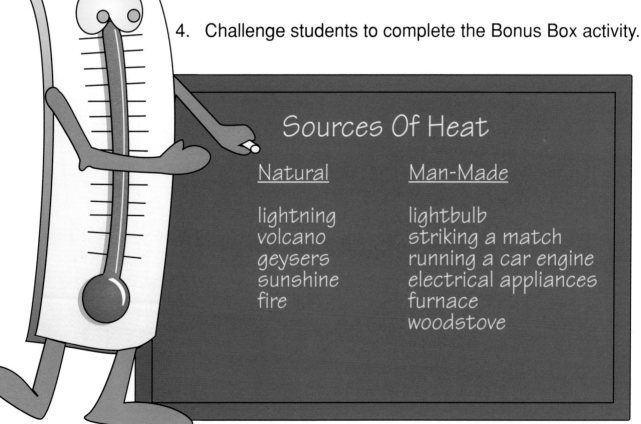

Sources Of Heat

Natural	Man-Made
lightning	lightbulb
volcano	striking a match
geysers	running a car engine
sunshine	electrical appliances
fire	furnace
	woodstove

Hot Stuff!

Heat can come from a *natural source,* such as a forest fire.
It can also come from a *man-made source,* such as a microwave.

Cut out each heat source below.
Glue each picture in the correct column.

Bonus Box: On the back of this sheet, list the different sources of heat you have used today.

Natural	**Man-Made**

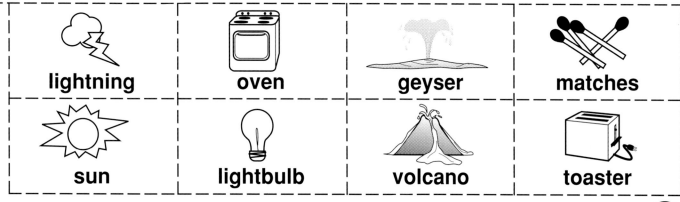

lightning   oven   geyser   matches

sun   lightbulb   volcano   toaster

How To Extend The Lesson:

- Challenge students to think about the many sources of heat they use each day. Assign each student a room of a house and have him list the different sources of heat often found in that room. Enlist students' help in compiling the findings onto a chart labeled "Heat In Our Homes."

- Show students what a powerful source of heat the sun is. Place each of two ice cubes in a separate, clear plastic cup. Leave one cup in the classroom and place the other outside in direct sunlight. Have students observe the two cups to see the difference in melting time.

- Divide students in pairs, and instruct each pair to name and write ten things that are associated with heat. Challenge each pair to use the words to create a word-search puzzle. Then have each twosome trade puzzles with another pair and find the words on that list.

- Have each student cut out pictures of heat sources from discarded magazines. Collect the pictures and place them in a decorated container. Duplicate a class supply of the heat-source cards below. Give each student one of each card. Have the student color his cards and glue them back-to-back with a craft stick between them. Then randomly draw a picture of a heat source from the container and show it to the class. Each student holds his craft stick so that the appropriate card is facing you. Continue in this manner until all the pictures have been drawn.

Patterns

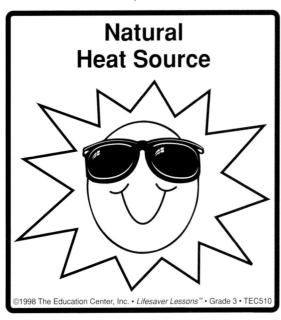

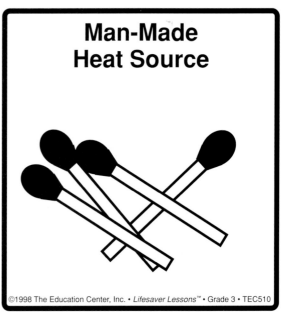

Fabulous Foods

Serve up this hearty lesson on the Food Guide Pyramid.
It's the perfect recipe to help your youngsters build healthful eating habits.

Skill: Understanding the Food Guide Pyramid

Estimated Lesson Time: 30 minutes

Teacher Preparation:
1. Duplicate page 81 for each student.
2. Enlarge a copy of the Food Guide Pyramid on page 80 and make a transparency of it. Or draw the Pyramid on the chalkboard.

Materials:
1 copy of page 81 per student
1 piece of scrap paper per student
overhead projector and transparency (or drawn copy) of the Food Guide Pyramid on page 80

Background Information:
The Food Guide Pyramid was developed by the U.S. Department of Agriculture to encourage people to improve their diets. It is an outline of what to eat every day. A range of servings is provided for each major group. The number of servings that a person needs depends on how many calories his body requires.

At the bottom of the Food Guide Pyramid is the largest group, *grains,* which consists of bread, cereal, pasta, and rice. This group should constitute the basis of our diets. These foods are good sources of fiber and energy. The next layer on the Pyramid consists of two groups: the fruits group and the vegetables group. The foods in both of these groups are important sources of vitamins and minerals. The dairy group includes all milk products, which are high in calcium and protein. The protein group contains meats, poultry, eggs, fish, dried peas, beans, and nuts. Foods in this group are high in protein. The foods at the top of the Food Guide Pyramid—fats, oils, and sweets—are high in calories and low in nutrients. They should be eaten sparingly.

Introducing The Lesson:

Ask your students to imagine that they are in charge of planning the school lunch menus. Then have each student write on a piece of scrap paper items he might serve for a school lunch.

Steps:

1. After students have written their menus, tell them that an important part of planning a menu is determining its nutritional content. Point to the displayed or illustrated copy of the Food Guide Pyramid. Then share the Background Information on page 79 with your students.

2. Ask your students to categorize their menu selections according to the Food Guide Pyramid. Explain that some foods, such as pizza and hamburgers, contain ingredients from several areas of the Pyramid. Have students determine whether they have a healthful balance of choices in their menu selections.

3. Next give each student a copy of the grocery list on page 81. Beside each food, have the student use the code to write the letters for its food group.

4. Challenge students to complete the Bonus Box activity.

Science
Fun Facts About

_____

by _____

Our class learned about _____
_____.
The most interesting fact I learned was
_____
_____
_____.

Fun Fact #1

_____
_____
_____
_____
_____

Fun Fact #3

_____
_____
_____
_____
_____

Fun Fact #2

_____
_____
_____
_____
_____

Fun Fact #4

_____
_____
_____
_____
_____

Fun Fact Illustration

What I learned is important because

_____
_____
_____
_____
_____.

89

How To Extend The Lesson:

- Create a class book about a science topic with facts from students' minibooks. Have each student create a page or an illustration for the class book. Then use the book as a unit review.

- Have students share their minibooks with another class that has been studying the same topic. Encourage the class members to quiz each other on the subject.

- Keep the minibooks handy for parent conferences. The personalized choice of information will show parents where students' strengths and interests are.

- Award each student with a personalized copy of the award pattern below.

Presenting an award to

_____
(student)

for great work during our study of

_____.

©1998 The Education Center, Inc. • *Lifesaver Lessons*™ • Grade 3 • TEC510

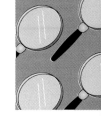

Professor Eggbert's Science Review

Crack open this sunny-side-up activity for an "egg-cellent" science review!

Skill: Reviewing science concepts

Estimated Lesson Time: 30 minutes

Teacher Preparation:

1. Duplicate page 93 for each student.
2. Create a large Professor Eggbert cutout similar to the one shown below.

Materials:
1 copy of page 93 per student
1 Professor Eggbert cutout
scissors
glue

Teacher Tip:
This activity can be used to reinforce a current unit of study or as a review of material discussed earlier in the school year.

Introducing The Lesson:

Show students the Professor Eggbert cutout. Tell students that Professor Eggbert would like to know some information about the current science topic they are studying (or about a unit previously studied). But the only way he can understand the information is if it is written on eggs.

Steps:

1. Ask students to brainstorm desired information about the science topic. Write students' responses on the chalkboard—at least one response per student.

2. Give each student a copy of page 93. On the cracked eggshell, have each student write the science topic on the top line and her name on the bottom line. Then have her choose at least three facts from the chalkboard and write them on the other egg.

3. Next have her cut on the heavy black lines, including the zigzag line. Finally ask her to put glue on the gray areas on the whole egg shape and place the two half egg shapes on top as shown.

4. After the glue dries, display the eggs and Professor Eggbert on a bulletin board titled "An 'Egg-cellent' Review."

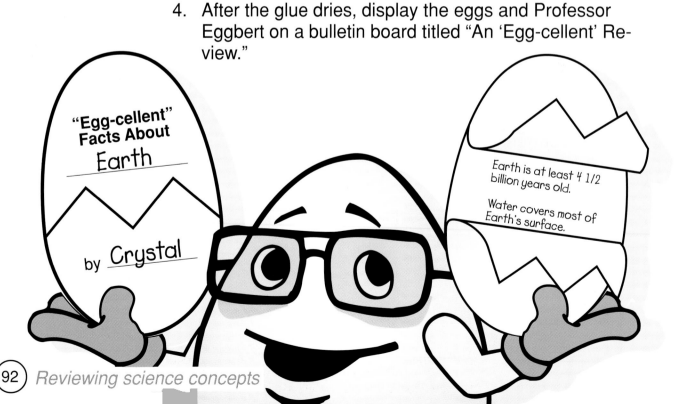

"Egg-cellent" Facts About Earth
by Crystal

Earth is at least 4 1/2 billion years old.

Water covers most of Earth's surface.

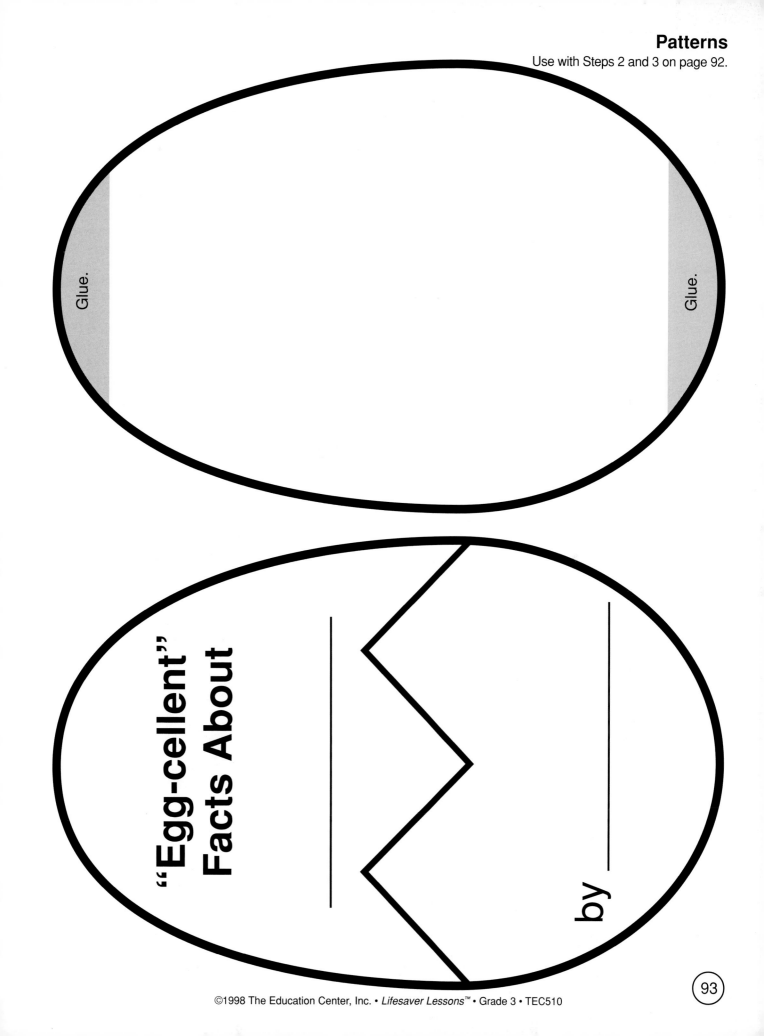

Glue.

Glue.

"Egg-cellent" Facts About

by

How To Extend The Lesson:

- Label one egg carton (or basket) "true" and another egg carton (or basket) "false." For each student, program a slip of paper with a fact or nonfact; then place each paper slip in a sealable plastic egg. Have each student open an egg and read aloud the information. Then have her tuck the fact back in the egg and place the egg in the corresponding carton (or basket). For an added challenge, have students reword the false statements to make them true.

- Divide the class into teams. Number each team; then label an egg carton for each team. Also place a class supply of plastic eggs in a basket. Have each team stand in a line parallel to the other teams. Beginning with Team One, ask the first student in line a question from the current science topic. If he answers correctly he puts a plastic egg in his team's egg carton. If he answers incorrectly, repeat the question to the first student in line on Team Two. Either way the student from Team One moves to the back of his line. Continue in this same manner until each student has a turn. The team that has the most eggs in its carton wins!

- Duplicate copies of the award shown below for your students.

Professor Eggbert's
Good Egg Award
is presented to

_____
(student)

for "egg-cellent"
work in science.

©1998 The Education Center, Inc. • *Lifesaver Lessons*™ • Grade 3 • TEC510

Reviewing science concepts

Answer Keys

Page 9
1. Force of 6 to 8
2. Force of 3 to 5
3. Force of 0 to 2
4. Force of 12 and above
5. Force of 6 to 8
6. Force of 9 to 11

Page 13
1. touch, metal
2. house, car, building
3. away, water
4. tree, hilltop
5. wet, ground
6. telephone, emergency

Page 21
1. anteater
2. duck
3. spider
4. snake
5. shark
6. bee
7. bat
8. eagle
9. frog
10. elephant

Page 45
(Answers will vary.)
1. There are changes in size and shape.
   Yes.
   It is a physical change.
2. There are changes in size, shape, color, texture, and substance.
   No.
   It is a chemical change.
3. There are changes in size and shape.
   Yes.
   It is a physical change.
4. There are changes in color and substance.
   No.
   It is a chemical change.
5. There are changes in color.
   Yes.
   It is a physical change.

Page 69
(The order of answers in each category may vary.)
Transparent: clean water, clear glass, plastic wrap, clean air
Translucent: waxed paper, paper towel, tissue paper, cloud
Opaque: cardboard, aluminum foil, wood, black poster board

Page 77
(The order of answers in each category may vary.)
Natural Heat Sources: lightning, sun, geyser, volcano
Man-Made Heat Sources: oven, lightbulb, matches, toaster

Page 81
1. P
2. G
3. V
4. F
5. P
6. D
7. F
8. V
9. G
10. D
11. G
12. V
13. F
14. P
15. FS
16. P
17. D or P
18. FS
19. V
20. G
21. P
22. FS

Page 85
1. Sugar Snaps
2. Sugar Snaps
3. Power Pops
4. Sugar Snaps
5. Power Pops
6. Power Pops
7. Power Pops; 6
8. Power Pops; It has fewer sugars; less fat; and more proteins, vitamins, and minerals.
   (Answers will vary for number 8.)

Grade 3 Science Management Checklist

SKILLS	PAGES	DATE(S) USED	COMMENTS
WEATHER			
Weather Terminology	3		
Wind Speed	7		
Rules For Weather Safety	11		
ANIMALS			
Life Cycles	15		
Animal Adaptations	19		
Classifying Vertebrates	23		
Amazing Animal Facts	27		
PLANETS			
Planet Order	31		
Researching Planets	35		
MATTER			
Classifying States Of Matter	39		
Changes In Matter	43		
EARTH			
Earth's Habitats	47		
Earth's Layers	51		
Rocks	55		
Signs Of Erosion	59		
SIMPLE MACHINES			
Identifying Simple Machines	63		
ENERGY			
Light	67		
Sound	71		
Sources Of Heat	75		
NUTRITION			
The Food Guide Pyramid	79		
Reading A Nutrition Label	83		
BASIC SCIENCE REVIEW			
Adaptable Fun Facts Minibook	87		
Open Review	91		